Scott Foresman
Science

The Diamond Edition

PEARSON
Scott Foresman

Editorial Offices: Glenview, Illinois • Parsippany, New Jersey • New York, New York
Sales Offices: Boston, Massachusetts • Duluth, Georgia • Glenview, Illinois
Coppell, Texas • Sacramento, California • Mesa, Arizona
www.pearsonsuccessnet.com

Series Authors

Dr. Timothy Cooney
Professor of Earth Science and Science Education
University of Northern Iowa (UNI)
Cedar Falls, Iowa

Dr. Jim Cummins
Professor
Department of Curriculum, Teaching, and Learning
University of Toronto
Toronto, Canada

Dr. James Flood
Distinguished Professor of Literacy and Language
School of Teacher Education
San Diego State University
San Diego, California

Barbara Kay Foots, M.Ed.
Science Education Consultant
Houston, Texas

Dr. M. Jenice Goldston
Associate Professor of Science Education
Department of Elementary Education Programs
University of Alabama
Tuscaloosa, Alabama

Dr. Shirley Gholston Key
Associate Professor of Science Education
Instruction and Curriculum Leadership Department
College of Education
University of Memphis
Memphis, Tennessee

Dr. Diane Lapp
Distinguished Professor of Reading and Language Arts in Teacher Education
San Diego State University
San Diego, California

Sheryl A. Mercier
Classroom Teacher
Dunlap Elementary School
Dunlap, California

Karen L. Ostlund, Ph.D.
UTeach Specialist
College of Natural Sciences
The University of Texas at Austin
Austin, Texas

Dr. Nancy Romance
Professor of Science Education & Principal Investigator
NSF/IERI Science IDEAS Project
Charles E. Schmidt College of Science
Florida Atlantic University
Boca Raton, Florida

Dr. William Tate
Chair and Professor of Education and Applied Statistics
Department of Education
Washington University
St. Louis, Missouri

Dr. Kathryn C. Thornton
Former NASA Astronaut Professor
School of Engineering and Applied Science
University of Virginia
Charlottesville, Virginia

Dr. Leon Ukens
Professor Emeritus
Department of Physics, Astronomy, and Geosciences
Towson University
Towson, Maryland

Steve Weinberg
Consultant
Connecticut Center for Advanced Technology
East Hartford, Connecticut

ISBN–13: 978-0-328-28957-8 (SVE), ISBN–10: 0-328-28957-4 (SVE);
ISBN–13: 978-0-328-30430-1 (A), ISBN–10: 0-328-30430-1 (A);
ISBN–13: 978-0-328-30431-8 (B), ISBN–10: 0-328-30431-X (B);
ISBN–13: 978-0-328-30432-5 (C), ISBN–10: 0-328-30432-8 (C);
ISBN–13: 978-0-328-30433-2 (D), ISBN–10: 0-328-30433-6 (D)

Copyright © 2008 Pearson Education, Inc.

All Rights Reserved. Printed in the United States of America. This publication is protected by Copyright, and permission should be obtained from the publisher prior to any prohibited reproduction, storage in a retrieval system, or transmission in any form by any means, electronic, mechanical, photocopying, recording, or otherwise. For information regarding permission(s), write to: Permissions Department, Scott Foresman, 1900 East Lake Avenue, Glenview, Illinois 60025.

4 5 6 7 8 9 10 V063 15 14 13 12 11 10 09 08
CC: N1

Consulting Author

Dr. Michael P. Klentschy
Superintendent
El Centro Elementary School District
El Centro, California

Science Content Consultants

Dr. Frederick W. Taylor
Senior Research Scientist
Institute for Geophysics
Jackson School of Geosciences
The University of Texas at Austin
Austin, Texas

Dr. Ruth E. Buskirk
Senior Lecturer
School of Biological Sciences
The University of Texas at Austin
Austin, Texas

Dr. Cliff Frohlich
Senior Research Scientist
Institute for Geophysics
Jackson School of Geosciences
The University of Texas at Austin
Austin, Texas

Brad Armosky
McDonald Observatory
The University of Texas at Austin
Austin, Texas

NASA Content Consultants

Adena Williams Loston, Ph.D.
Chief Education Officer
Office of the Chief Education Officer

Clifford W. Houston, Ph.D.
Deputy Chief Education Officer for Education Programs
Office of the Chief Education Officer

Frank C. Owens
Senior Policy Advisor
Office of the Chief Education Officer

Deborah Brown Biggs
Manager, Education Flight Projects Office
Space Operations Mission Directorate, Education Lead

Erika G. Vick
NASA Liaison to Pearson Scott Foresman
Education Flight Projects Office

William E. Anderson
Partnership Manager for Education
Aeronautics Research Mission Directorate

Anita Krishnamurthi
Program Planning Specialist
Space Science Education and Outreach Program

Bonnie J. McClain
Chief of Education
Exploration Systems Mission Directorate

Diane Clayton, Ph.D.
Program Scientist
Earth Science Education

Deborah Rivera
Strategic Alliances Manager
Office of Public Affairs
NASA Headquarters

Douglas D. Peterson
Public Affairs Officer, Astronaut Office
Office of Public Affairs
NASA Johnson Space Center

Nicole Cloutier
Public Affairs Officer, Astronaut Office
Office of Public Affairs
NASA Johnson Space Center

Dr. Jennifer J. Wiseman
Hubble Space Telescope Program Scientist
NASA Headquarters

Reviewers

Dr. Maria Aida Alanis
Administrator
Austin ISD
Austin Texas

Melissa Barba
Teacher
Wesley Mathews Elementary
Miami, Florida

Dr. Marcelline Barron
Supervisor/K-12 Math
and Science
Fairfield Public Schools
Fairfield, Connecticut

Jane Bates
Teacher
Hickory Flat Elementary
Canton, Georgia

Denise Bizjack
Teacher
Dr. N. H. Jones Elementary
Ocala, Florida

Latanya D. Bragg
Teacher
Davis Magnet School
Jackson, Mississippi

Richard Burton
Teacher
George Buck Elementary
School 94
Indianapolis, Indiana

Dawn Cabrera
Teacher
E.W.F. Stirrup School
Miami, Florida

Barbara Calabro
Teacher
Compass Rose Foundation
Ft. Myers, Florida

Lucille Calvin
Teacher
Weddington Math &
Science School
Greenville, Mississippi

Patricia Carmichael
Teacher
Teasley Middle School
Canton, Georgia

Martha Cohn
Teacher
An Wang Middle School
Lowell, Massachusetts

Stu Danzinger
Supervisor
Community Consolidated
School District 59
Arlington Heights, Illinois

Esther Draper
Supervisor/Science Specialist
Belair Math Science
Magnet School
Pine Bluff, Arkansas

Sue Esser
Teacher
Loretto Elementary
Jacksonville, Florida

Dr. Richard Fairman
Teacher
Antioch University
Yellow Springs, Ohio

Joan Goldfarb
Teacher
Indialantic Elementary
Indialantic, Florida

Deborah Gomes
Teacher
A J Gomes Elementary
New Bedford, Massachusetts

Sandy Hobart
Teacher
Mims Elementary
Mims, Florida

Tom Hocker
Teacher/Science Coach
Boston Latin Academy
Dorchester, Massachusetts

Shelley Jaques
Science Supervisor
Moore Public Schools
Moore, Oklahoma

Marguerite W. Jones
Teacher
Spearman Elementary
Piedmont, South Carolina

Kelly Kenney
Teacher
Kansas City Missouri
School District
Kansas City, Missouri

Carol Kilbane
Teacher
Riverside Elementary School
Wichita, Kansas

Robert Kolenda
Teacher
Neshaminy School District
Langhorne, Pennsylvania

Karen Lynn Kruse
Teacher
St. Paul the Apostle
Yonkers, New York

Elizabeth Loures
Teacher
Point Fermin
Elementary School
San Pedro, California

Susan MacDougall
Teacher
Brick Community Primary
Learning Center
Brick, New Jersey

Jack Marine
Teacher
Raising Horizons Quest
Charter School
Philadelphia, Pennsylvania

Nicola Micozzi Jr.
Science Coordinator
Plymouth Public Schools
Plymouth, Massachusetts

Paula Monteiro
Teacher
A J Gomes Elementary
New Bedford, Massachusetts

Tracy Newallis
Teacher
Taper Avenue Elementary
San Pedro, California

Dr. Eugene Nicolo
Supervisor, Science K-12
Moorestown School District
Moorestown, New Jersey

Jeffry Pastrak
School District of Philadelphia
Philadelphia, Pennslyvania

Helen Pedigo
Teacher
Mt. Carmel Elementary
Huntsville Alabama

Becky Peltonen
Teacher
Patterson Elementary School
Panama City, Florida

Sherri Pensler
Teacher/ESOL
Claude Pepper Elementary
Miami, Florida

Virginia Rogliano
Teacher
Bridgeview Elementary
South Charleston, West
Virginia

Debbie Sanders
Teacher
Thunderbolt Elementary
Orange Park, Florida

Grethel Santamarina
Teacher
E.W.F. Stirrup School
Miami, Florida

Migdalia Schneider
Teacher/Bilingual
Lindell School
Long Beach, New York

Susan Shelly
Teacher
Bonita Springs Elementary
Bonita Springs, Florida

Peggy Terry
Teacher
Madison Elementary
South Holland, Illinois

Jane M. Thompson
Teacher
Emma Ward Elementary
Lawrenceburg, Kentucky

Martha Todd
Teacher
W. H. Rhodes Elementary
Milton, Florida

Renee Williams
Teacher
Bloomfield Schools
Central Primary
Bloomfield, New Mexico

Myra Wood
Teacher
Madison Street Academy
Ocala, Florida

Marion Zampa
Teacher
Shawnee Mission
School District
Overland Park, Kansas

Science

See learning in a whole new light

Unit A Life Science

What do living things need?

Chapter 1 • Living and Nonliving

Chapter 2 • Habitats

Where do plants and animals live?

Unit A Life Science

How do parts help living things?

Chapter 3 • How Plants and Animals Live

Chapter 4 • Life Cycles

How do animals and plants grow and change?

Unit A Life Science

How are living things connected?

Chapter 5 • Food Chains

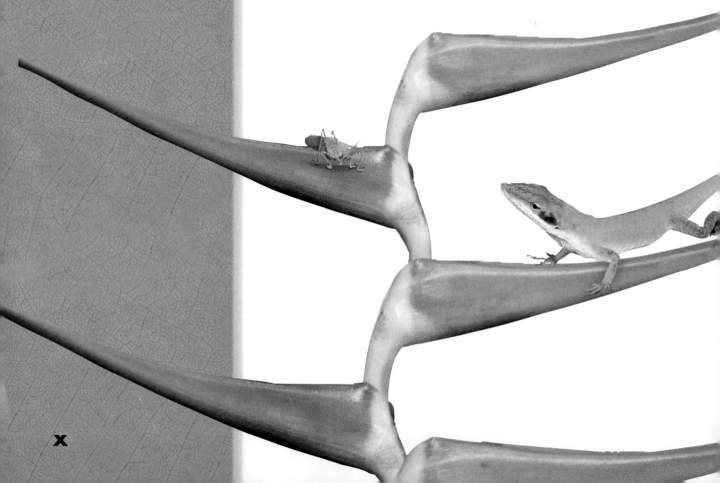

Unit B Earth Science

How are land, water, and air important?

Chapter 6 • Land, Water, and Air

Chapter 7 • Weather

What are the four seasons?

Unit C Physical Science

How can objects be described?

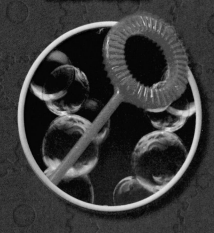

Chapter 8 • Observing Matter

Chapter 9 • Movement and Sound

What makes objects move?

Unit C · Physical Science

Where does energy come from?

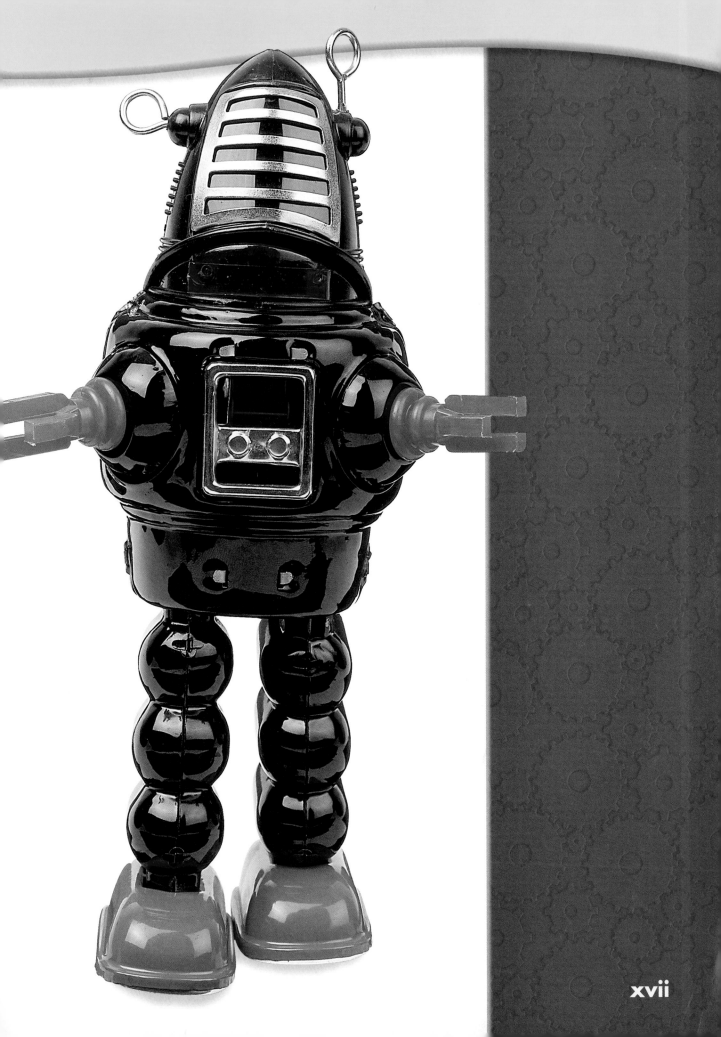

What is in
the sky?

Chapter 11 • Day and Night Sky

Chapter 12 • Science in Our World

How does technology help people?

How to Read Science

Each chapter in your book has a page like this one. This page shows you how to use a reading skill.

Before reading

First, read the Build Background page. Next, read the How To Read Science page. Then, think about what you already know. Last, make a list of what you already know.

Target Reading Skill

The target reading skill will help you understand what you read.

Real-World Connection

Each page has an example of something you will learn.

Graphic Organizer

A graphic organizer can help you think about what you learn.

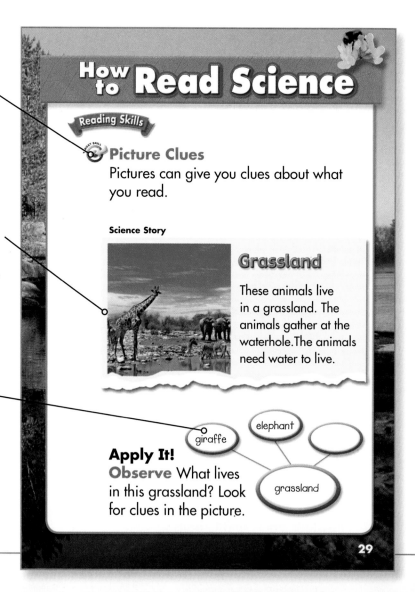

How to Read Science

Reading Skills

Picture Clues

Pictures can give you clues about what you read.

Science Story

Grassland

These animals live in a grassland. The animals gather at the waterhole. The animals need water to live.

Apply It!
Observe What lives in this grassland? Look for clues in the picture.

giraffe · elephant · grassland

29

Map Facts
A swamp is a wetland. Okefenokee Swamp in Georgia has about 70 islands.

crane

dragonfly

bullfrog

Lesson Checkpoint
1. What does a duck get in a wetland?
2. Use **picture clues** to tell what animals live in a wetland.

35

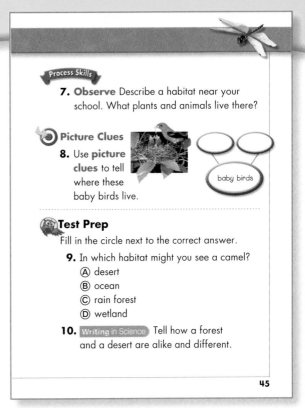

Process Skills

7. **Observe** Describe a habitat near your school. What plants and animals live there?

Picture Clues

8. Use **picture clues** to tell where these baby birds live.

baby birds

Test Prep
Fill in the circle next to the correct answer.

9. In which habitat might you see a camel?
    Ⓐ desert
    Ⓑ ocean
    Ⓒ rain forest
    Ⓓ wetland

10. Writing in Science Tell how a forest and a desert are alike and different.

45

During reading

Use the checkpoint as you read the lesson. This will help you check how much you understand.

After reading

Think about what you have learned. Compare what you learned with the list you made before you read the chapter. Answer the questions in the Chapter Review.

Target Reading Skills

These are some target reading skills that appear in this book.

- Cause and Effect
- Alike and Different
- Put Things in Order
- Predict
- Draw Conclusions
- Picture Clues
- Important Details

Science Process Skills

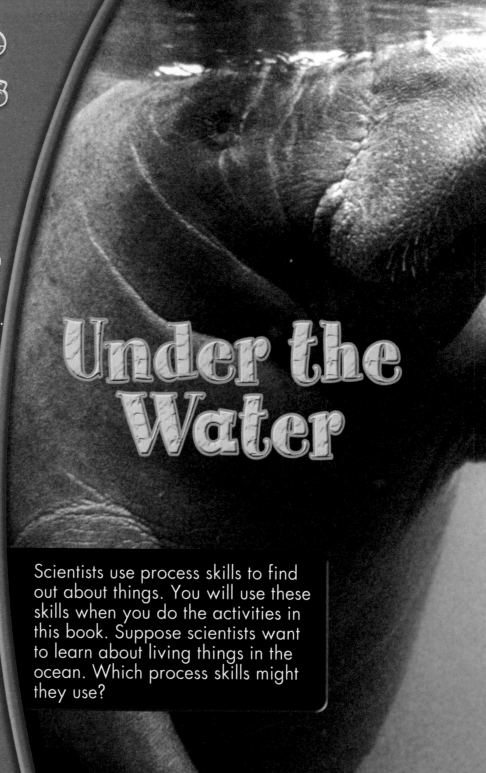

Observe
A scientist who wants to find out about the ocean observes many things. You use your senses to find out about things too.

Classify
Scientists classify living things in the ocean. You classify when you sort or group things by their properties.

Estimate and Measure
Scientists can estimate the size of living things in the ocean. This means they make a careful guess about the size or amount of something. Then they measure it.

Infer
Scientists are always learning about living things in the ocean. Scientists draw a conclusion or make a guess from what they already know.

Under the Water

Scientists use process skills to find out about things. You will use these skills when you do the activities in this book. Suppose scientists want to learn about living things in the ocean. Which process skills might they use?

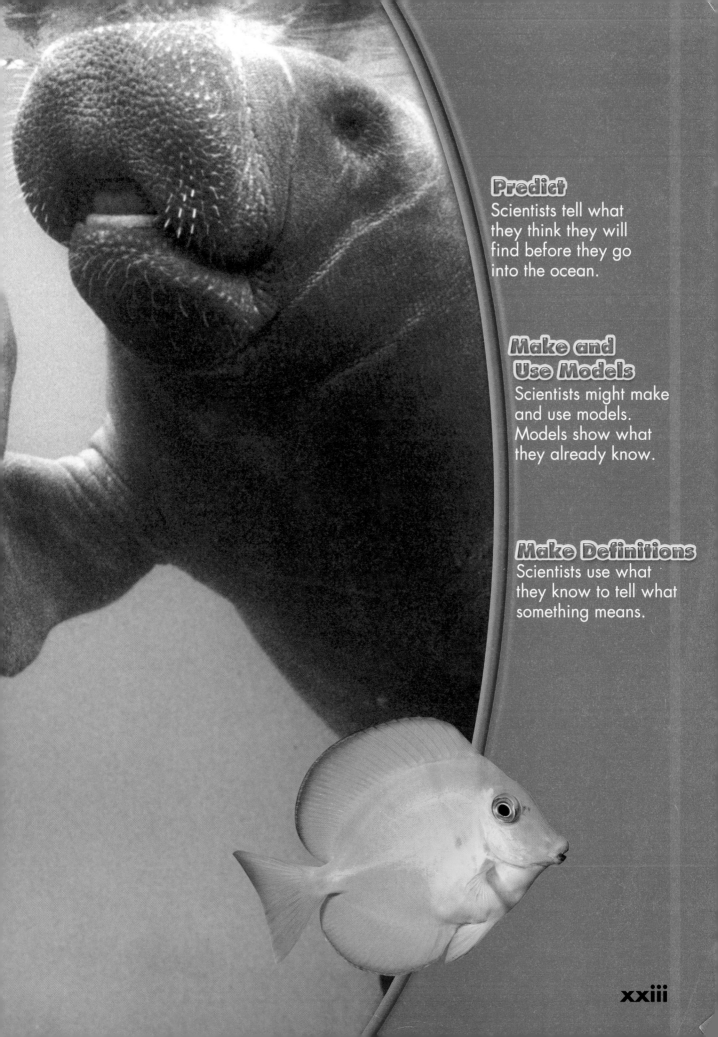

Predict
Scientists tell what they think they will find before they go into the ocean.

Make and Use Models
Scientists might make and use models. Models show what they already know.

Make Definitions
Scientists use what they know to tell what something means.

Science Process Skills

Make Hypotheses

Think of a question you have about living things in the ocean. Make a statement that you can test to answer your question.

Suppose you were a scientist. You might want to learn more about the ocean. What questions might you have? How would you use process skills to help you learn?

Collect Data

Scientists record what they observe and measure. Scientists put this data into charts or graphs.

Interpret Data

Scientists use what they learn to solve problems or answer questions.

Investigate and Experiment

Scientists plan and do an investigation as they study the ocean.

Control Variables

Scientists plan a fair test. Scientists change only one thing in their test. Scientists keep everything else the same.

Communicate

Scientists tell what they learn about living things in the ocean.

Using Scientific Methods

Scientific methods are ways of finding answers. Scientific methods have these steps. Sometimes scientists do the steps in a different order. Scientists do not always do all of the steps.

Ask a question.

Ask a question that you want answered.

Do seeds need water to grow?

Make your hypothesis.

Tell what you think the answer is to your question.

If seeds are watered, then they will grow.

Plan a fair test.

Change only one thing.

Keep everything else the same.

Water one pot with seeds.

no water   water

Do your test.

Test your hypothesis. Do your test more than once. See if your results are the same.

Collect and record your data.

Keep records of what you find out. Use words or drawings to help.

Tell your conclusion.

Observe the results of your test. Decide if your hypothesis is right or wrong. Tell what you decide.

Seeds need water to grow.

no water

water

Go further.

Use what you learn. Think of new questions or better ways to do a test.

Ask a Question

Make Your Hypothesis

Plan a Fair Test

Do Your Test

Collect and Record Your Data

Tell Your Conclusion

Go Further

Science Tools

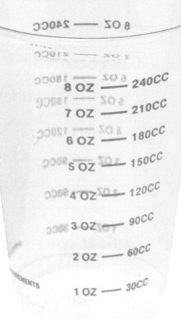

| 8 OZ — 240CC |
| 7 OZ — 210CC |
| 6 OZ — 180CC |
| 5 OZ — 150CC |
| 4 OZ — 120CC |
| 3 OZ — 90CC |
| 2 OZ — 60CC |
| 1 OZ — 30CC |

Scientists use many different kinds of tools.

Measuring cup
You can use a measuring cup to measure volume. Volume is how much space something takes up.

Stopwatch
A stopwatch measures how much time something takes.

Computer
You can learn about science at a special Internet website. Go to www.pearsonsuccessnet.com.

Ruler
You can use a ruler to measure how long something is. Most scientists use a ruler to measure length in centimeters or millimeters.

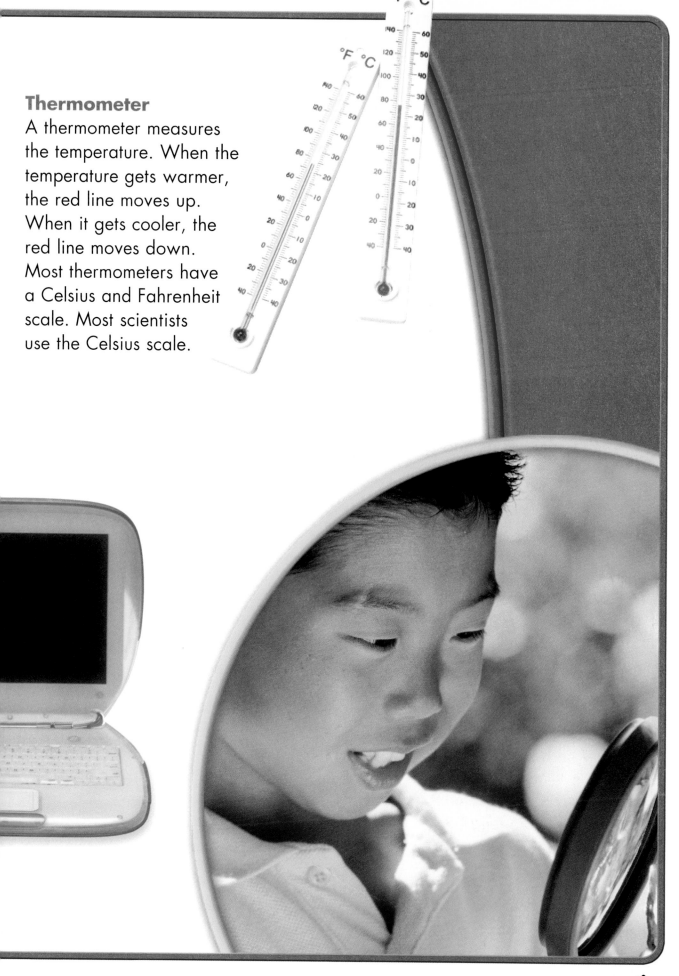

Thermometer

A thermometer measures the temperature. When the temperature gets warmer, the red line moves up. When it gets cooler, the red line moves down. Most thermometers have a Celsius and Fahrenheit scale. Most scientists use the Celsius scale.

Science Tools

Safety goggles
You can use safety goggles to protect your eyes.

Calculator
A calculator can help you do things, such as add and subtract.

Balance
A balance is used to measure the mass of objects. Mass is how much matter an object has. Most scientists measure mass in grams or kilograms.

Meterstick
You can use a meterstick to measure how long something is too. Scientists use a meterstick to measure in meters.

Clock
A clock measures time.

Hand lens
A hand lens makes objects look larger.

N S

N

S

...agnet
...u can use a magnet to
...e if an object is made of
...rtain metals.

Safety in Science

You need to be careful when doing science activities. This page includes safety tips to remember:

- Listen to your teacher's instructions.
- Never taste or smell materials unless your teacher tells you to.
- Wear safety goggles when needed.
- Handle scissors and other equipment carefully.
- Keep your work place neat and clean.
- Clean up spills immediately.
- Tell your teacher immediately about accidents or if you see something that looks unsafe.
- Wash your hands well after every activity.

Chapter 8
Observing Matter

online
Student Edition
pearsonsuccessnet.com

Discovery Channel School
Student DVD

You Will Discover
- ways that matter can be grouped.
- ways that matter can change.

How can objects be described?

liquid

matter

gas

mass

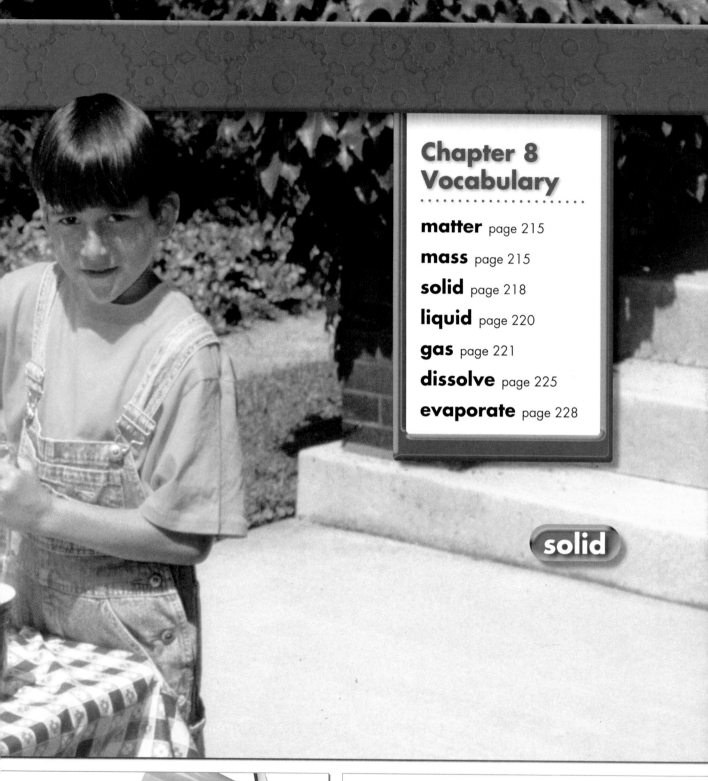

Chapter 8 Vocabulary

solid

dissolve

evaporate

Evaporate means to change from a liquid to a gas.

Explore What is in the bags?

Materials

1 2 3 4 5

5 bags with classroom objects

What to Do

1 Take turns reaching into each bag. Touch, smell, and listen.

2 Predict what is in each bag.

3 Look in the bags. Did you predict correctly?

Process Skills

You can **communicate** how touching, smelling, and listening help you predict what is in the bags.

Explain Your Results

Communicate How does touching help you predict?

How to Read Science

 Alike and Different

Alike means how things are the same. Different means how things are not the same.

Science Story

Lemons and Lemonade

The lemon is yellow and bumpy. The lemon tastes sour. The lemonade is yellow and tastes sweet. The lemonade can spill.

Apply It!

Communicate Tell how the lemon and the lemonade are alike and different.

Alike	Different

A "Matter" of Lemonade

Sung to the tune of "Turkey in the Straw"
Lyrics by Gerri Brioso & Richard Freitas/The Dovetail Group, Inc.

When you're making lemonade
you use lemons and cups,
And a great big pitcher that
you will fill up.
Each one has its own shape
and it takes up space.
All are solid kinds of matter
you can find anyplace.

Science Songs

Lesson 1

What is matter?

The pitcher is made of matter.
The drink is made of matter.

Matter is anything that takes
up space.
Matter has many tiny parts.
Matter has mass.

Mass is the amount of matter
in an object.
Everything made of matter has mass.

The lemon is made of matter. Some parts of matter are too small to see without a hand lens.

Describing Matter

The things in the picture
are made of matter.
What shapes do you see?
What colors do you see?
How are the things
alike and different?

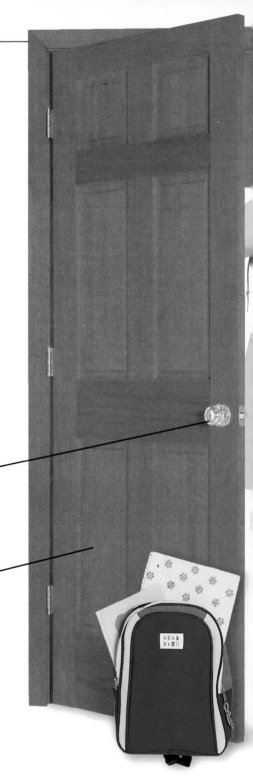

**The door handle
is made of metal.**

**The wood door is a rectangle.
The door feels hard.**

✓ **Lesson Checkpoint**

1. What are two ways you can group
   the things in the picture?

2. **Writing** in Science
   Make a chart like this one.
   Fill it in with words that
   tell about each thing.

	Color	Feel
door		
scarf		
basket		
boots		

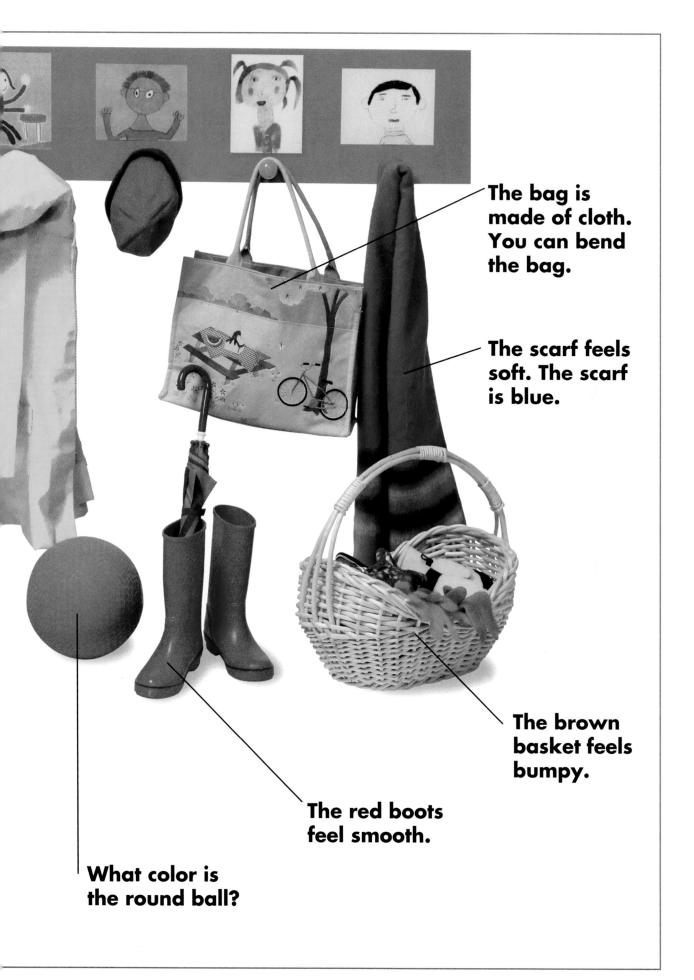

The bag is made of cloth. You can bend the bag.

The scarf feels soft. The scarf is blue.

The brown basket feels bumpy.

The red boots feel smooth.

What color is the round ball?

Lesson 2

What are solids, liquids, and gases?

What toys do you see?
All of the toys are solids.

A **solid** takes up space.
A solid has its own shape.
A solid does not change shape
when it is moved from place to place.

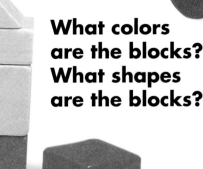

**What colors
are the blocks?
What shapes
are the blocks?**

1. ✔Checkpoint What is a solid?

2. 🔄 Choose two solids from the picture.
How are the solids **alike and different**?

Liquids and Gases

A liquid can change shape.
A **liquid** takes the shape of
its container.
A liquid takes up space.
A liquid is matter.

Look at the different shapes a liquid can take.

A **gas** can change size and shape.
Gas takes up space.
Gas takes the shape of its container.

Gas takes the size and shape of the ball.

Air is a gas.
Air is all around us.
Air is matter.

The bubbles are filled with air.

✔ **Lesson Checkpoint**

1. What is one way to group the matter on these pages?

2. 🎯 How are solids and liquids **alike and different**?

Lesson 3

How does matter change?

Matter can be changed in many different ways. Look at how things in the picture have changed.

A whole apple has one shape. Apples can be cut into new shapes.

The straw was straight. Now it is bent.

The shape of the bread changed.

A liquid can be cooled until it freezes.
A solid can be heated until it melts.
Find something in the picture that
is melting.

Hurry!
Put the popsicle
in the cooler.

The popsicle
is melting.

1. ✅ Checkpoint How can matter be changed?

2. 🎯 How are the whole apple and the cut apple **alike and different**?

Mixing Solids and Liquids

You can mix some matter.
Look at the soup.
The soup has different solids.
The soup has a liquid.

The solids are mixed with
the liquid. You can take
the solids out of the liquid.

**The carrots
are solids.**

**The noodles
are solids.**

**The chicken
is a solid.**

**The broth
is a liquid.**

Some solids dissolve in liquids. **Dissolve** means to spread throughout a liquid.

The salt will dissolve in the water. This makes salt water.

✓**Lesson Checkpoint**

1. What happens when a solid dissolves?

2. **Writing in Science** Tell what solids you might put in a salad. Tell what liquid you might mix with your salad.

Lesson 4

How can water change?

Water is a liquid.
Water freezes when it gets very cold.
The water changes to ice.

Ice is a solid.
Heat melts ice.
The ice changes to water.

Ice is frozen water.
Ice feels cold
and hard.

Water boils when it gets very hot.
Heat changes the water to a gas.
The gas is called water vapor.
You cannot see water vapor.

The water inside the pot is boiling. Steam is coming out of the pot. Steam is water vapor that is given off when water boils.

1. 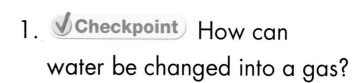 How can water be changed into a gas?

2. **Technology** in Science What do people use to boil water?

Water Can Evaporate

The ground is wet.
What will happen to the water?

Some of the water on the ground will evaporate. **Evaporate** means to change from a liquid to a gas.

The water on the ground can change to water vapor.

Water in an open container will disappear. Water in a closed container will not disappear.

Heat from sunlight causes the water in the puddle to evaporate.

✓ Lesson Checkpoint

1. What happens to water that evaporates?

2. Writing in Science In your **science journal,** write about what will happen to a puddle on a hot day.

229

Lesson 5

What are other ways matter changes?

Sometimes one kind of matter
changes into a different kind of matter.
It will not change back to the way it was.

**Iron in part of the table
has changed to rust.**

**The apple's color
will not change
back.**

Paper can burn.
Paper changes into ashes when it burns.
Ashes will not change back into paper.

People can use paper to start a campfire.

The paper will burn.

The paper turns into ashes when it is burned.

✓ **Lesson Checkpoint**

1. How can paper change?

2. **Math in Science** Suppose you had three apples. Each apple was cut into two pieces. How many pieces of apple would you have? Write a number sentence.

Investigate Will it float or sink?

Materials

classroom objects

tub with water

What to Do

1 Choose an object.

2 Predict Will it float or sink?

Be careful!

Clean up spills right away.

3 Put the object in the water. Does it float or sink?

Process Skills

When you **classify**, you sort things that are alike and different.

④ Try the other objects.

⑤ **Collect data** in the chart.

Sink or Float?		
Object	**Predict**	**What happens?**
eraser	float	sink

Explain Your Results

1. **Classify** Which objects float and which objects sink?
2. Why do you think some objects float and others sink?

Go Further

Would the same objects float or sink in salt water? Try it and find out.

Comparing Height and Weight

Orange juice is a liquid. The cup, the bottle, and the jug all hold orange juice. Compare their heights.

List the bottle, cup, and jug in order from tallest to shortest.

Bottle   **Cup**   **Jug**

Orange

Watermelon

Cherry

An orange, a watermelon, and a cherry are solids.

Look at the pictures of the orange, watermelon, and cherry. Compare their weights.

List the orange, watermelon, and cherry in order from lightest to heaviest.

Lab zone Take-Home Activity

Find three solid objects. Put the objects in order from lightest to heaviest. Draw a picture to show the order.

Vocabulary

Which picture goes with each word?

1. solid
2. liquid
3. gas

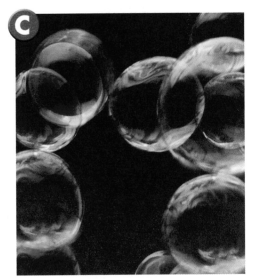

What did you learn?

4. How are solids and liquids alike and different?

5. Look around you. Name an object you can see. What are three ways to describe it?

6. What are four ways matter can change?

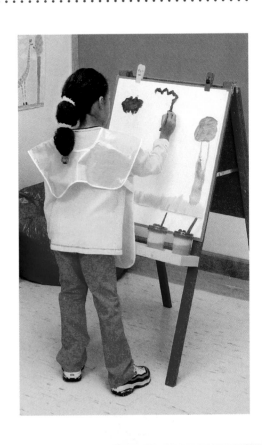

7. Classify Take five objects out of your desk. What is one way you can group the objects? Now group them in a different way.

Alike and Different

8. How are the balls **alike and different**?

Alike	Different

Test Prep

Fill in the circle next to the correct answer.

9. What happens to water when it boils?

   Ⓐ It changes to a solid.

   Ⓑ It changes to a gas.

   Ⓒ It changes to a liquid.

   Ⓓ It dissolves.

10. Writing in Science Write a sentence. Tell what happens when you mix salt and water.

Matter on the Moon

Look up in the sky at night.
You can see the Moon.
Astronauts from NASA
have walked on the Moon.

Matter weighs more on
Earth than on the Moon.

How many pounds does a book bag weigh?

Pounds

10
9
8
7
6
5
4
3
2
1
0

Book bag on Earth

Book bag on the Moon

Lab zone **Take-Home Activity**

Draw a picture of yourself on the Moon. Show your picture to your family. Tell them if you would weigh more or less on the Moon.

Blowing Glass

Read Together

Glass is a solid.
Fire can change glass.
Glass melts when it gets very hot!
Fire makes glass very hot and soft.

Glassblowers use glass to make
things such as bowls and vases.
Glassblowers put hot glass at one
end of a long tube.
They blow into the other end.
Then they use tools to shape the glass.

**Dale Chihuly is
a glassblower.**

Lab
zone **Take-Home Activity**

Place a balloon on one
end of a cardboard tube.
Use tape to hold it in place.
Blow into the other end of
the tube. Describe what
happens to your balloon.

Chapter 9

Movement and Sound

online
Student Edition
pearsonsuccessnet.com

What makes objects move?

force

gravity

speed

magnet

attract

Chapter 9 Vocabulary

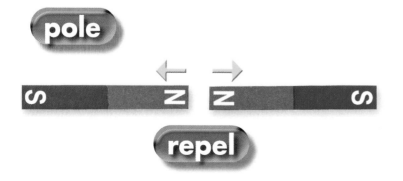

pole

repel

vibrate

Vibrate means to move back and forth very fast.

Be careful!

Explore How can you move the car?

Wear your safety goggles.

Materials

safety goggles

rubber band

2 pencils

toy car

What to Do

1 Have your partners stretch a rubber band between 2 pencils.

2 Put the car next to the rubber band.

3 Pull the rubber band back. Let go. Observe.

What pushes the car?

Hold each pencil in place.

Process Skills

Predict means to tell what you think might happen.

Explain Your Results

Predict What would happen if you pulled the rubber band farther back?

Cause and Effect

A cause is why something happens. An effect is what happens.

Science Story

Moving a Wagon
The girl can use the wagon to move her toy.

Apply It!

Suppose the girl starts pulling the wagon. **Predict** what effect that will have on the wagon.

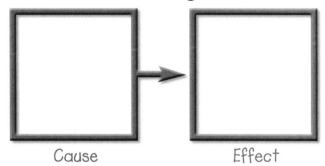

Cause   Effect

Pull the Sled!

Sung to the tune of "Three Blind Mice"
Lyrics by Gerri Brioso & Richard Freitas/The Dovetail Group, Inc.

Pull the sled.

Pull the sled.

Pull it up the hill.

Pull it up the hill.

Don't let go or you soon will see

The sled sliding down 'cause of gravity.

To get it back up you must certainly,

Pull the sled!

Lesson 1

What makes things move?

The children use force to move the sled to the top of the hill.

Force is a push or a pull that may make something move.

Suppose the children let go of the sled.

Whoosh! Gravity pulls the sled down the hill. **Gravity** is a force that pulls things toward the ground.

Using Force

The children use a little force to pull the sleds over the snow. The girl in the picture below uses a lot of force to move the heavy snow.

Suppose the girl drops the shovel. Gravity will pull it to the ground.

These children use force to move the sleds over the snow.

✓ **Lesson Checkpoint**

1. What is gravity?

2. **Writing** in Science Write in your **science journal.** Tell how the children use force to make the sled move.

Lesson 2

What is speed?

Force can change the way things move. The child pushes the car with a lot of force. The car moves quickly.

The car has a lot of speed. **Speed** is how quickly or slowly something moves.

The child pushes the car with less force. The car will move at a slower speed.

☑ **Lesson Checkpoint**

1. What is speed?

2. **Cause and Effect** What causes the car to have a lot of speed?

The boy pushes the car.

**The car slows down.
The car stops.**

The girl can push the car in another direction.

251

Lesson 3

How do things move?

Things can move up and down.
Things can move left and right.
Things can move in a straight
line or in a circle.

Things can even
move in a zigzag.
How do the things
in these pictures move?

**First, the marble
rolls down the
orange bar. Then,
it zigzags down
the other bars.**

**The metal balls move
back and forth.**

The cars follow the path of the track.
First, the cars move around one curve.
Next, the cars go straight.
Then, the cars move around
another curve.

**The cars go around and
around the track.**

1. ✓Checkpoint What are some
   ways things can move?

2. **Math** in Science Count how
   many bars the marble will
   roll down.

Different Places

Look at the block tower.
Find the long red block.
How many blocks are above
the red block?
How many blocks are below
the red block?

Find the block next to the tower.
What color is the block?

**This orange block
is between two
yellow blocks.**

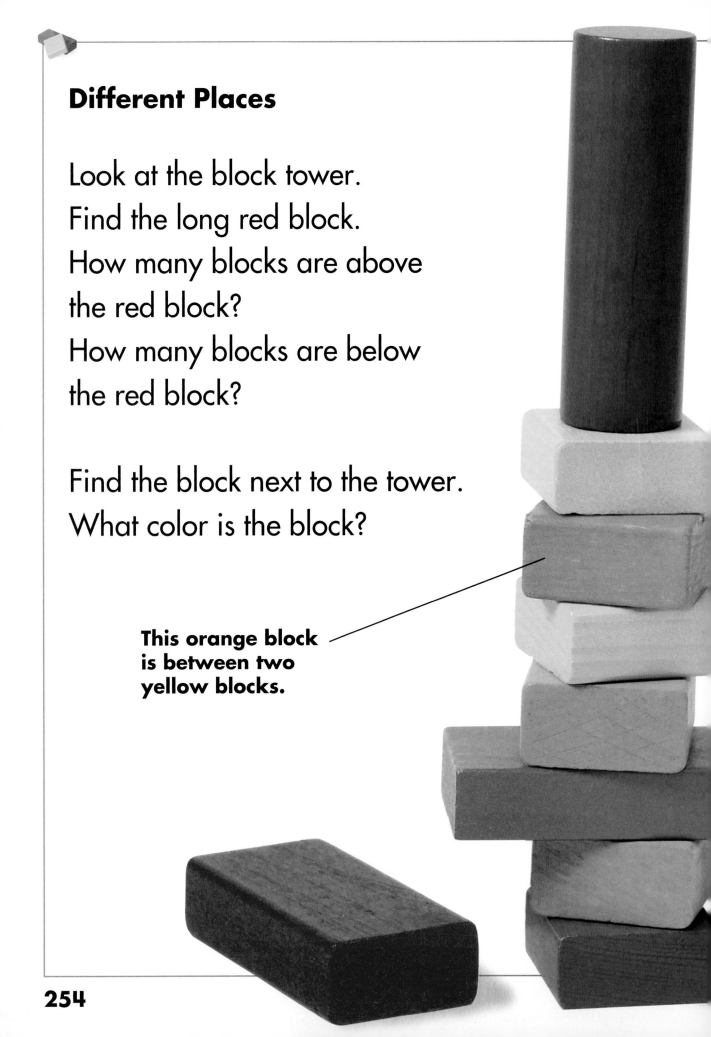

Crash!
Look at what can happen if you pull out the bottom block.

1. Write in your **science journal.** Tell what is above you, below you, and next to you.

2. 🎯 **Cause and Effect**
   Suppose you move the orange block in the tower. How might this affect the blocks next to the orange block?

What do magnets do?

What holds the train cars together?
Magnets do!

A **magnet** is an object that attracts some kinds of metal.
Attract means to pull toward.

N stands for north pole. S stands for south pole.

A magnet has two poles.
A **pole** is at the end of some magnets.
Every magnet has a north pole
and a south pole.

Different poles attract each other. A north pole and a south pole attract each other.

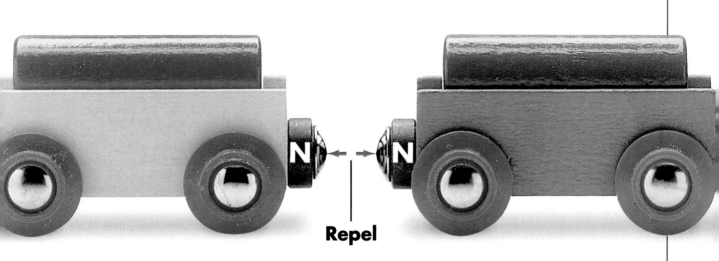

Repel

Suppose you turn one train car around.
Now two north poles are by each other.
The two north poles repel each other.
Repel means to push away.
Poles that are the same will repel each other.

1. ✓Checkpoint When do magnets attract each other?

2. Writing in Science Write a sentence. Tell what will happen if you put two south poles together.

Pulling Metal

Look at the objects in the basket.
What will the magnet attract?
The magnet will attract things
made of iron.
Iron is one kind of metal.

The magnet attracts this iron lock.

The penny does not have iron in it. The magnet does not attract a penny.

A magnet can pull on an object made of iron without touching it. The magnet pulls more on an object when it is close to the object.

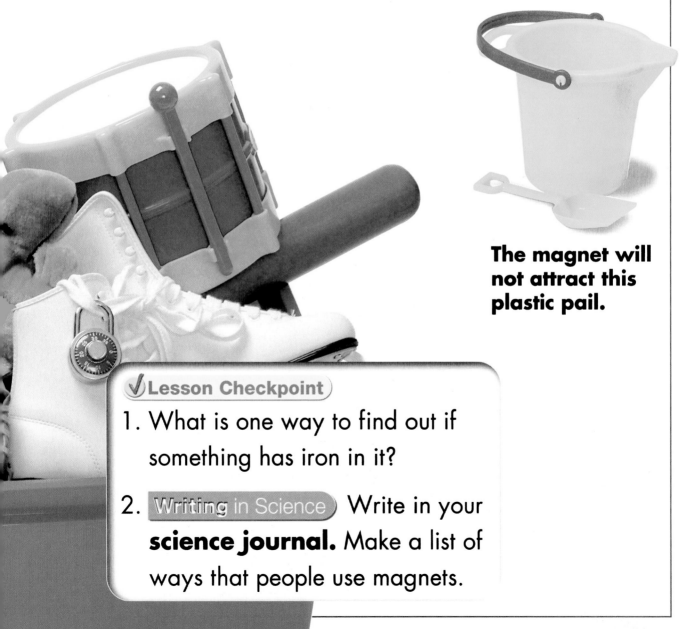

The magnet will not attract this plastic pail.

✓ Lesson Checkpoint

1. What is one way to find out if something has iron in it?

2. Writing in Science Write in your **science journal.** Make a list of ways that people use magnets.

Lesson 5

How are sounds made?

When a sound is made something vibrates. **Vibrate** means to move back and forth very fast.

Pluck a banjo string. It sounds soft. Pluck the string harder. It sounds loud.

The banjo strings vibrate when you pluck them. The vibrations make sounds.

Give the top of the drum a gentle tap. The top of the drum will vibrate. The top of the drum will make a soft sound.

✓ **Lesson Checkpoint**

1. How does a banjo make a sound?

2. **Health** in Science Loud sounds can hurt your ears. What might you do to protect your ears?

Lesson 6

What sounds are around us?

Suppose you were on this street. What sounds might you hear?

You might hear sirens.
You might hear honks.
You might hear beeps.

Honks, beeps, and sirens tell us to be careful.

Zoom!
Look up! What makes that sound in the sky?

1. ✔️ Checkpoint Describe two sounds that can help you.

2. **Technology** in Science Name three machines and the sounds they make.

Sounds of Nature

Many things in nature make sounds.
Look at these pictures.
What sounds might you hear?

✓ Lesson Checkpoint

1. What sounds in nature might be loud?

2. **Social Studies** in Science What sounds might you hear in your neighborhood?

Chirp! Chirp!

That chirping sounds like baby birds.

Clap!

That loud clap
sounds like thunder.

How might
the falling
water
sound?

Crash!

That crashing
sounds like
waves hitting
the rocks.

How might
falling leaves
sound?

265

Investigate What do you hear?

Materials

safety goggles

plastic cup and
rubber band

paper cup with
hole in bottom

string and paper clip

cup with water

Process Skills

You **infer** when
you answer a
question using
what you have
learned.

What to Do

1 Make your first
noisemaker. Stretch
a rubber band
around the plastic cup.

2 Hold the bottom of
the cup to your ear.
Pluck the rubber band
gently. Listen. Record
what you hear.

Be careful!

Wear your
goggles!

3 Make your second
noisemaker.
Push the string
through the hole
in the cup.

4 Tie the paper clip on the outside of the cup. Wet the string.

5 Hold the cup. Pull down on the wet string with your fingers. Listen. Record what you hear.

Noisemaker	Does it sound like a duck 🦆 or a guitar 🎸?

Explain Your Results

1. **Infer** Why do you think you hear the different sounds?

2. What instruments do you know that vibrate?

Go Further

What sound would you hear if you use a dry string? Try it and find out.

Speed

Moving At Different Speeds

slowest ➔ slower ➔ slow

Use the pictures to answer the questions.
1. What two things are faster than a car?
2. What is slower than a turtle?

fast ➜ **faster** ➜ **fastest**

Lab
zone **Take-Home Activity**

Find pictures of six things that move. Put them in order from slowest to fastest.

Vocabulary

Which picture goes with each word?

1. attract
2. pole
3. repel

What did you learn?

4. What makes things move?

5. What force pulls things toward the ground?

6. What are three different ways that things can move?

7. What is speed?

8. How are sounds made?

9. Infer What might happen if you hit the top of a drum hard?

Cause and Effect

10. You cause a bike to move by pushing the pedals. Suppose you push harder. What effect will that have on how the bike moves?

Cause → Effect

Test Prep

Fill in the circle next to the correct answer.

11. What happens to magnets if you try to touch their south poles to each other?
- (A) They attract.
- (B) They vibrate.
- (C) They repel.
- (D) They pull.

12. Writing in Science Write two sentences. Tell what happens when magnets attract and repel some things.

Dr. Shamim Rahman

Read Together

Shamim Rahman was six years old when he saw an astronaut walk on the moon. Since then, he has always wanted to be a rocket scientist.

Now Dr. Rahman is a rocket scientist at NASA. Rockets help the space shuttle move into space. Dr. Rahman works to build and test newer and better rockets.

Dr. Rahman is on a team that checks the rocket engines before the shuttle takes off.

Lab zone Take-Home Activity

Scientists send rockets into space to take pictures of Earth. Draw what you think Earth would look like from space. Explain your picture to your family.

Chapter 10
Learning About Energy

online **Student Edition**
pearsonsuccessnet.com

Web Games
Take It to the Net
pearsonsuccessnet.com

You Will Discover

- that there are different kinds of energy.
- ways that people use energy.

Where does energy come from?

energy

heat

fuel

electricity

274

Chapter 10 Vocabulary

shadow

battery

Explore Can the Sun's light heat water?

Materials

2 thermometers

2 cups with cold water

temperature chart

red crayons

Process Skills

You **infer** when you draw a conclusion to answer a question.

What to Do

1 Put 1 thermometer in each cup. Record the temperatures.

2 Put 1 cup in a sunny place. Put the other cup in a shady place.

3 Wait 2 hours. Record the temperatures on your temperature chart.

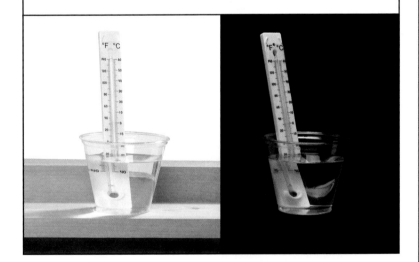

Explain Your Results

Infer Why did one cup have warmer water after 2 hours?

TARGET SKILL

Draw Conclusions

You draw conclusions when you decide something about what you see and read.

Science Story

Playing Outside

Mark uses Sunlight
to read.
It is now late in the day.
Mark turns on the light.

Apply It!
Infer Why does Mark turn on the light?

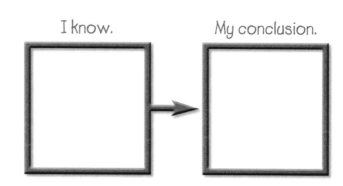

I know.

My conclusion.

Energy

Sung to the tune of "My Bonnie"
Lyrics by Gerri Brioso & Richard Freitas/The Dovetail Group, Inc.

I sit on the beach in the summer.
The Sun is up high in the sky.
The light from the Sun heats
the beach sand.
Just ask me and I'll tell you why.

Lesson 1

What gives off heat?

Heat comes from the light of the Sun.
Heat moves from warmer places to cooler places.
Heat moves from warmer objects to cooler objects.

Light from the Sun warms the land.
Light from the Sun warms the water.
Light from the Sun warms the air.

Heat

Look at the picture.
Heat comes from the fire.
The heat warms the food.
The heat warms the air.

Fire was used to heat the marshmallow.

The girl is drinking hot cocoa to warm up. Heat comes from the hot cocoa.

Rub your hands together.
Rubbing things together makes heat.
The heat from rubbing your hands
together makes them warm.

Heat comes from other things too.
Heat comes from lamps, stoves,
and toasters.
What else can give off heat?

✔ **Lesson Checkpoint**

1. What are five things that heat
   comes from?

2. 🎯 **Draw Conclusions** What
   would happen to Earth without the Sun?

Lesson 2

What can energy do?

Light is a form of energy. **Energy** can change things. Energy from the Sun can change the temperature.

It is a sunny day. Things with light colors feel cool. Things with dark colors feel warm.

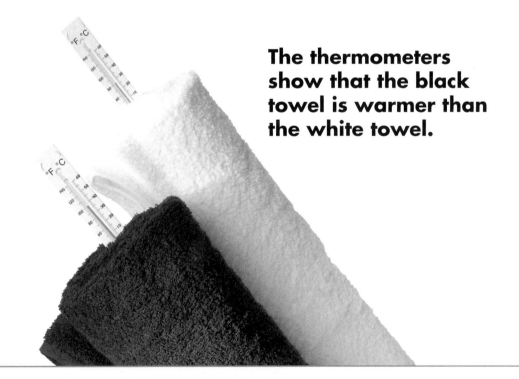

The thermometers show that the black towel is warmer than the white towel.

In summer, many people like to wear clothes with lighter colors. Lighter colors take in less energy from the Sun.

✔️Lesson Checkpoint

1. What can energy from the Sun do?

2. 🎯 **Draw Conclusions** What color could you wear to stay cool on a sunny summer day?

Lesson 3

What makes light and shadows?

Look at the light around you.
Is the light from the Sun?
Is the light from a fire?

Light comes from both of these things.
Light comes from stars and candles too.
Where else does light come from?

Light can shine through thin colored paper.

Light comes from light bulbs. The light bulbs shine in the dark room.

See the firefly's light. The firefly shines in the dark.

1. ✓Checkpoint What are some things that give off light?

2. Writing in Science Write two sentences in your **science journal.** Tell about the lights you see at night.

Making Shadows

Light passes through some things.
Light will pass through a
window. Light will not pass
through everything. Light will
not pass through you.

Shine the flashlight on the toy.
The toy blocks the light.
The toy makes a shadow.
A **shadow** is made
when something blocks
the light.

**Look at the shadow
the toy robot makes.**

A shadow is large when the light is close. A shadow is small when the light is far away.

1. ✓Checkpoint What causes a shadow?

2. Art in Science Make a shadow on white paper. Have a friend trace the shadow.

morning

noon

Look at the tree's shadow in the morning.

Look at the shadow at noon. The shadow is shorter.

Changing Shadows

The tree blocks the Sun's light.
The tree makes a shadow.
Shadows are long when the
Sun seems low in the sky.

The Sun seems to move during the day.
The Sun is high in the sky at noon.

late in day

Look at the tree's shadow late in the day.

It is late in the day.
Now the shadow is in a different place.

✓ **Lesson Checkpoint**

1. How does a tree's shadow change from morning to night?

2. **Math** in Science Measure a shadow in the morning and at noon. Which is longer?

Lesson 4

What uses energy around us?

Most cars get energy from fuel. **Fuel** is anything that is burned to make heat or power.

Cars use gasoline as a fuel. The car's engine burns the fuel. Now the car has the energy to move.

Electricity makes lights in a walk sign work.

The lights in the sign change.

SciLinks Take It to the Net
pearsonsuccessnet.com   keyword: electricity
code: g1p290

Cars use fuel to move.

The streetlight uses electricity to shine at night.

1. ✓Checkpoint How does a car get energy to move?

2. **Writing** in Science Tell how you use lights each day.

Using Energy

How does the fan get energy?
The fan gets energy from electricity.

Electricity moves through power
lines into a building.
Electricity moves from the outlet
through the cord.

Now the fan has energy.
Turn the fan on.
The fan blades move.

**What kind of energy
do these things use?**

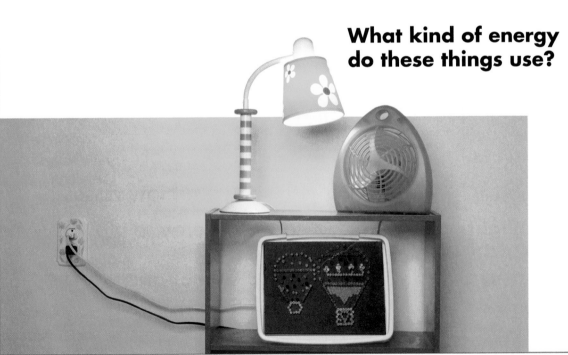

Suppose you put the batteries in the toy. Now turn on the toy. The toy will move!

A battery stores energy. A **battery** changes the energy to electricity. The toy uses the electricity to move.

✓ Lesson Checkpoint

1. How does electricity get to the fan?

2. **Technology** in Science Name two machines that use batteries.

293

How do you get energy?

Yum! What foods do you see?
You get energy from food.
You need energy to move.
You need energy to grow and change.

milk

cheese

Milk and cheese help you grow strong teeth and bones.

fruit

Bread and cereal give you energy to play.

bread and cereal

Energy helps your body
in many ways.

meat

**Meat helps your body
grow. Meat helps your
body repair itself.**

**Fruits and vegetables
help your body work
the way it should.**

vegetables

1. ✓**Checkpoint** Where do you
get energy?

2. **Health** in Science Why do you
need energy?

295

When You Use Energy

You use energy all day long.
You use energy when you move.
You use energy when you play.

You use energy when you sit.
You use energy to turn the pages
of a book.

You even use energy when you sleep.
You need energy for everything you do.

✓ **Lesson Checkpoint**

1. Why do you need energy while you sleep?

2. Writing in Science In your **science journal,**
   make a list of 6 things you do that use
   energy.

You use energy when you swim.

You think when you read. Thinking takes energy too!

You use energy to hop from square to square.

Your body is growing and changing even when you sleep. Growing and changing take energy.

Investigate How can you make a shadow?

Materials

flashlight and
white paper

marker

eraser

plastic bag

plastic cup

book

What to Do

1 **Predict** Which objects
will make a dark shadow?
Record **yes** or **no.**

2 Shine a light on white paper.
Hold an object in front of
the paper.

Process Skills

You **predict** by
making a guess
based on what
you know.

Be careful! Do not shine the
light in eyes.

③ Observe Did it make a dark shadow?
Record **yes** or **no.**

Object	Predict	Observe
	Will it make a dark shadow?	Did it make a dark shadow?

Explain Your Results

Infer Why do some objects make a dark shadow and others do not?

┌─ **Go Further** ─
How can you change the size of a shadow? Make a plan to find out.

Reading a Picture Graph

Look at the graph. The graph shows how many servings Max should eat each day.

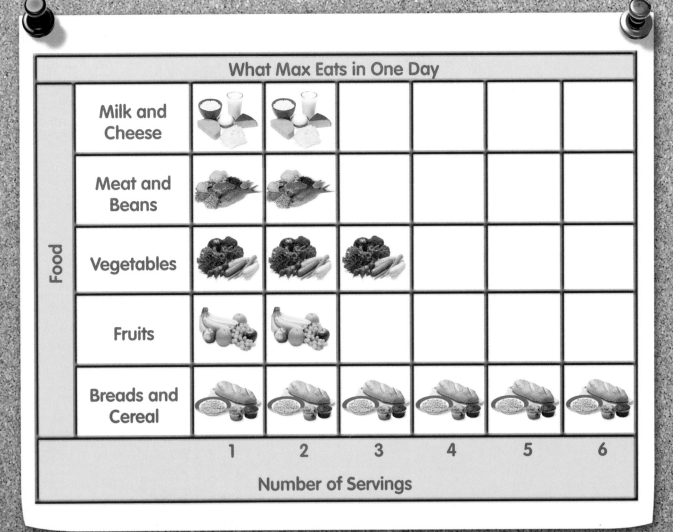

What Max Eats in One Day

Food

| Food | 1 | 2 | 3 | 4 | 5 | 6 |

Milk and Cheese

Meat and Beans

Vegetables

Fruits

Breads and Cereal

Number of Servings

Use the picture graph to answer the questions.
1. How many servings of milk and cheese does Max eat in one day?
2. How many servings of vegetables and fruits does Max eat in one day?

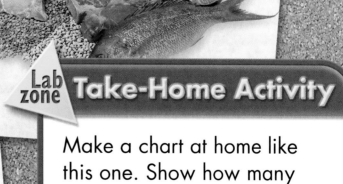

Lab zone Take-Home Activity

Make a chart at home like this one. Show how many servings of each food you eat in one day.

Vocabulary

Which picture goes with each word?

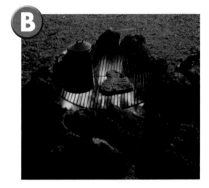

1. heat
2. shadow
3. fuel
4. battery

What did you learn?

5. What does electricity do?

6. What warms the land, the water, and the air?

7. How does a tree's shadow change during the day?

8. Infer What might you see if you shine a flashlight on a toy car?

Lunch

Draw Conclusions

9. Why did Shawn want to eat a healthful lunch? **Draw Conclusions.**

I know. → My conclusion.

Shawn was getting ready for a soccer game. She wanted to eat a healthful lunch.

Test Prep

Fill in the circle next to the correct answer.

10. How does food help you?

   Ⓐ It blocks the Sun.

   Ⓑ It gives you energy.

   Ⓒ It makes you tired.

   Ⓓ It uses energy.

11. **Writing in Science** Write a sentence about how you use energy at home.

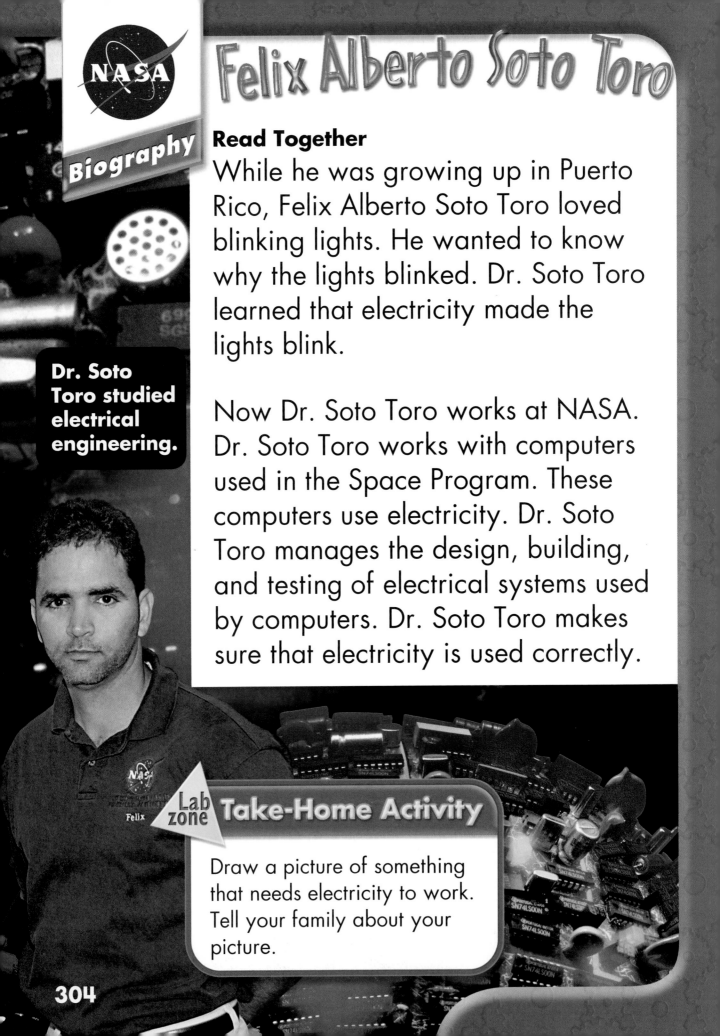

Felix Alberto Soto Toro

Read Together

While he was growing up in Puerto Rico, Felix Alberto Soto Toro loved blinking lights. He wanted to know why the lights blinked. Dr. Soto Toro learned that electricity made the lights blink.

Dr. Soto Toro studied electrical engineering.

Now Dr. Soto Toro works at NASA. Dr. Soto Toro works with computers used in the Space Program. These computers use electricity. Dr. Soto Toro manages the design, building, and testing of electrical systems used by computers. Dr. Soto Toro makes sure that electricity is used correctly.

Felix

Lab zone Take-Home Activity

Draw a picture of something that needs electricity to work. Tell your family about your picture.

Unit C Test Talk

Test-Taking Strategies

Find Important Words

▷ Choose the Right Answer

Use Information from Text and Graphics

Write Your Answer

Choose the Right Answer

Remove wrong answers to help you choose the right answer.

Nam uses force to move his toys.
Nam pulls his wagon.
Nam pushes his truck.

Read the question.

What kind of force does Nam use to move his truck?

    Ⓐ push

    Ⓑ energy

    Ⓒ motion

    Ⓓ pull

Your answer should be a kind of force.
Find the two answers that are kinds of forces.
Which one answers the question?

Unit C Wrap-Up

Chapter 8

How can objects be described?
- Objects can be described by their color and shape.
- Objects can be described by how they feel and what they are made of.

Chapter 9

What makes objects move?
- A force such as a push or a pull can make things move.
- A force called gravity pulls things to the ground.

Chapter 10

Where does energy come from?
- The Sun gives light energy and warms the land, water, and air.
- Fuel and electricity give energy to make things work.

Performance Assessment

Make a Song Using Different Sounds

- Find different objects in your classroom.
- Use objects to make quiet and loud sounds.
- Use the different sounds to make a song.

Play the song for a friend. Have your friend describe the sounds in the song.

Read More About Physical Science!

Look for books like these in your library.

Experiment How can you make high and low sounds?

What happens if you blow across the tops of bottles with different amounts of water? Experiment to find out.

Materials

3 bottles

funnel

2 cups with water

Ask a question.
Do bottles with different amounts of water make different sounds?

Make a hypothesis.
If you blow across the tops of bottles, do bottles with less water make higher or lower sounds?

Plan a fair test.
Make sure all the bottles are the same size.

Do your test.

1 Pour water into one bottle. Use the funnel.

Process Skills

You make a **hypothesis** to answer a question.

2 Pour water into the other bottles. Use the funnel.

3 Blow across the top of each bottle. Listen to each sound.

half full   less than half full   almost empty

4 Describe the sounds. Fill in the chart.

Collect and record data.

Is the sound high, medium, or low?

Bottle	Sound
Half full	
Less than half full	
Almost empty	

Tell your conclusion.

Did the bottles with less water make higher or lower sounds? What would you hear if you used an empty bottle?

Go Further

What will happen if you tap the bottles gently with a pencil? Experiment to find out.

Merry-Go-Round

by Dorothy Baruch

I climbed up on the merry-go-round,
And it went round and round.
I climbed up on a big brown horse
And it went up and down.

Around and round
And up and down,
Around and round
And up and down
I sat high up
On a big brown horse
And rode around
On the merry-go-round.

Science Fair Projects

Full Inquiry

Using Scientific Methods
1. Ask a question.
2. Make a hypothesis.
3. Plan a fair test.
4. Do your test.
5. Record and collect data.
6. Tell your conclusion.
7. Go further.

Idea 1

Energy in an Aquarium

Plan a project.

Find out how the light from the Sun can change the water in an aquarium.

Idea 2

Energy in a Terrarium

Plan a project.

Find out how animals in a terrarium get energy.

Metric and Customary Measurement

Science uses the metric system to measure things. Metric measurement is used around the world. Here is how different metric measurements compare to customary measurement.

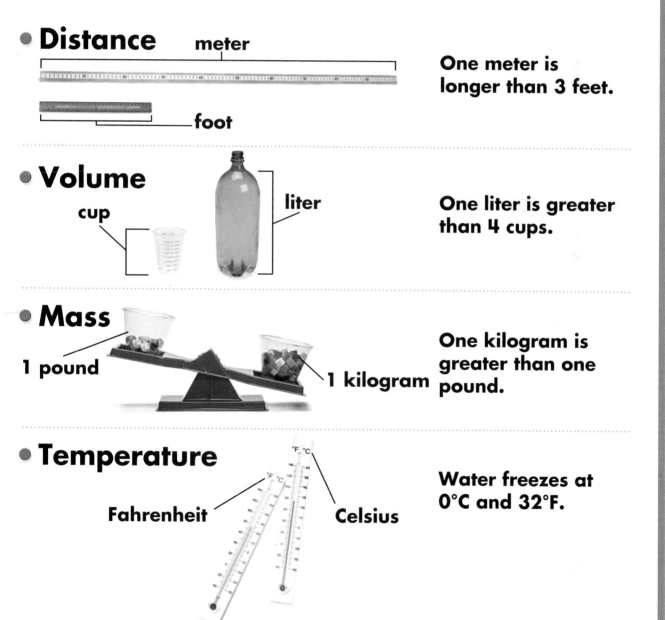

- **Distance**

meter

foot

One meter is longer than 3 feet.

- **Volume**

cup

liter

One liter is greater than 4 cups.

- **Mass**

1 pound

1 kilogram

One kilogram is greater than one pound.

- **Temperature**

Fahrenheit

Celsius

Water freezes at 0°C and 32°F.

Glossary

The glossary uses letters and signs to show how words are pronounced. The mark ′ is placed after a syllable with a primary or heavy accent. The mark ′ is placed after a syllable with a secondary or lighter accent.

To hear these words pronounced, listen to the AudioText CD.

Pronunciation Key

a in hat	ō in open	sh in she
ā in age	ȯ in all	th in thin
â in care	ô in order	ŦH in then
ä in far	oi in oil	zh in measure
e in let	ou in out	ə = a in about
ē in equal	u in cup	ə = e in taken
ėr in term	ů in put	ə = i in pencil
i in it	ü in rule	ə = o in lemon
ī in ice	ch in child	ə = u in circus
o in hot	ng in long	

alike (ə līk′) How things are the same. The two foxes look **alike**. (pages 5, 53, 96, 213)

antennae (an ten′ē) Feelers that help some animals know what is around them. **Antennae** help the crab feel, smell, and taste. (page 56)

Antennae

attract (ə trakt′) Attract means to pull toward. Magnets **attract** some objects. (page 256)

B

battery (bat′ər ē) Something that stores energy. The toy robot uses a **battery** to move. (page 293)

C

camouflage (kam′ə fläzh) A color or shape that makes an animal or plant hard to see. **Camouflage** helps the rabbit stay safe in its environment. (page 62)

cause (kȯz) Why something happens. Taking out the bottom block can cause the tower to fall. (pages 245, 254)

clay (klā) A soft part of soil that looks like mud, is sticky when wet, and is hard when dry. The **clay** felt sticky when Tanya touched it. (page 156)

cloud (kloud) A form in the air made of many tiny drops of water or pieces of ice when water vapor cools. We watched the fluffy, white **clouds** float overhead. (page 186)

desert (dez′ərt) A desert is a very dry habitat that gets little rain. Many **deserts** are hot during the day. (page 38)

different (dif′ər ənt) How things are not the same. The dogs are different colors. (pages 5, 53, 96, 213)

dissolve (di zolv′) To spread throughout a liquid. Salt will **dissolve** in water. (page 225)

draw conclusions

(dró kən klü′zhənz) When you decide something about what you see or read. You can **draw** a **conclusion** about what the shark will eat. (pages 117, 277)

effect (ə fekt′) What happens. The **effect** of pulling out the bottom block was that the blocks fell down. (pages 245, 254)

electricity (i lek′tris′ə tē) Makes things work. The streetlight uses **electricity** to shine. (page 290)

energy (en′ər jē) Something that can change things. Sunlight is a form of **energy** from the Sun. (page 282)

erosion (i rō′zhən) Happens when wind or water moves rocks and soil from one place to another. **Erosion** washed away the soil near the stream. (page 158)

evaporate (i vap′ə rāt′) To change from a liquid to a gas. The water on the ground quickly **evaporated** when the Sun came out. (page 228)

F

flower (flou′ər) The part of a plant that makes seeds. Our garden has many colorful **flowers**. (page 69)

food chain (füd chān) The way food passes from one living thing to another. All living things are connected through **food chains.** (page 125)

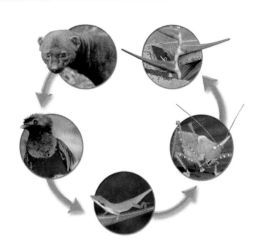

force (fôrs) A push or pull that makes objects move. The children used **force** to move the sled. (page 247)

forest (fôr′ist) A habitat with many trees and other types of plants. Many animals live in the **forest**. (page 31)

fuel (fyü′əl) Anything that is burned to make heat or power. People use gasoline as a **fuel** for cars. (page 290)

G

gas (gas) A kind of matter that can change size and shape. The bubbles are full of **gas**. (page 221)

gravity (grav′ə tē) A force that pulls things toward the ground. **Gravity** pulls falling leaves toward the ground. (page 247)

H

habitat (hab′ə tat) A place where plants and animals live. A deer lives in a forest **habitat**. (page 31)

heat (hēt) Moves from warmer places and objects to cooler places and objects. The **heat** from the campfire kept us warm. (page 279)

humus (hyü′ məs) A nonliving material made up of parts of living things that have died. Grandmother adds **humus** to the soil to help her plants grow. (page 156)

important details (im pôrt′nt di tālz′) Pictures and words that tell you about something. We looked for **important details** in the book we were reading. (pages 149, 317)

inclined plane (in klīnd′ plān) A simple machine that is high at one end and low at the other. It helps move things up and down. The builders used an **inclined plane** to help move the wood. (page 359)

larva (lär′və) A young insect that has a different shape from the adult. A butterfly **larva** is called a caterpillar. (page 92)

leaf (lēf) A part of a plant that makes food for the plant. A **leaf** fell from the rose bush. (page 69)

lever (lev′ər) A simple machine that can be used to lift something. Denny used a **lever** to lift the nail out. (page 358)

life cycle (līf sī′kəl) The changes that take place as a plant or an animal grows and changes. The **life cycle** of a frog includes an egg, a tadpole, and a grown frog. (page 90)

liquid (lik′wid) Matter that takes the shape of its container. Water is a **liquid**. (page 220)

living (liv′ing) Things that are alive and can grow and change. The butterfly is a **living** thing. (page 7)

magnet (mag′nit) An object that attracts some kinds of metal. A **magnet** can pull an object made of iron without touching it. (pages 256, 258)

marsh (märsh) A wetland habitat. Many different plants and animals live in a **marsh**. (page 126)

mass (mas) Amount of matter in an object. Everything made of matter has **mass**. (page 215)

matter (mat′er) Anything that takes up space. Everything around you is made of **matter**. (page 215)

mineral (min′ər əl) A nonliving material that can be found in rocks and soil. Copper is a **mineral**. (page 164)

Moon (mün) An object in the sky that moves around Earth. The **Moon** was shining brightly in the night sky. (page 326)

 N

natural resource

(nach′ər əl ri sôrs′) A useful thing that comes from nature. Rocks are a **natural resource**. (page 155)

nonliving (non liv′ing) Things that are not alive, don't grow, and don't change on their own. Tables and chairs are **nonliving** things. (page 14)

ocean (ō′shən) A large, deep habitat that has salt water. Some fish live in an **ocean** habitat. (page 36)

oxygen (ok′sə jən) A gas in the air that plants and animals need to live. Most living things need **oxygen** to live. (page 121)

planet (plan′it) A large body of matter that moves around the Sun. Earth is a **planet**. (page 324)

pole (pōl) At the end of some magnets. The north **pole** of one magnet will attract the south **pole** of another magnet. (page 256)

predict (pri dikt′) To make a guess from what you already know. See the clouds high in the sky. What do you **predict** the weather will be like? (page 181)

pulley (pul′ē) A simple machine that uses a wheel and rope to move things up and down. The workers used a **pulley** to move the wood. (page 358)

pupa (pyü′pə) The step after larva in some insects' life cycle. The hard covering of the **pupa** protects the caterpillar while it changes into a butterfly. (page 92)

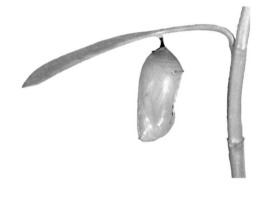

R

rain forest (rān fôr′ist) A habitat that gets a lot of rain. Plants with large green leaves grow in the **rain forest**. (page 122)

repel (ri pel′) To push away. The north poles of two magnets placed together will **repel** each other. (page 257)

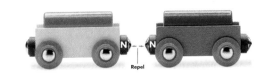

rocks (roks) Nonliving things that come from Earth. José collects **rocks**. (page 154)

root (rüts) Part of a plant that holds the plant in place and takes in water for the plant. We covered the **roots** of the rose plant with soil. (page 68)

rotation (rō tā′shən) The act of turning around and around. Earth's **rotation** causes day and night. (page 322)

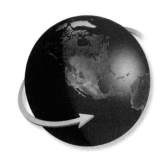

sand (sand) Tiny pieces of broken rock. We made castles of **sand** at the beach. (page 154)

screw (skrü) A simple machine used to hold things together. A **screw** was used to keep the two wooden boards together. (page 358)

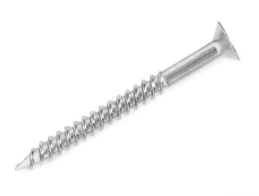

season (sē′zn) One of the four parts of the year. Winter is my favorite **season**. (page 192)

seed coat (sēd kōt) The protective shell that covers and protects a seed. The **seed coat** breaks open as the plant begins to grow. (page 98)

seedling (sēd′ling) A very young plant. Rafiq planted the **seedling** in his yard. (page 98)

shadow (shad′ō) A dark shape made when something blocks light. The toy made a **shadow** on the floor. (page 286)

shelter (shel′tər) A safe place for animals and people. This wolf pup uses an old log for **shelter**. (page 12)

simple machine (sim′pəl mə shēn′) A tool with few or no moving parts that does work. The wheel and axle of this wheelbarrow is a **simple machine**. (page 356)

sleet (slēt) Sleet is frozen rain. **Sleet** made the roads very slippery. (page 189)

solid (sol′id) A kind of matter that takes up space and has its own shape. A wooden block is a **solid**. (page 218)

speed (spēd) How quickly or slowly something moves. The car moved at a very fast **speed**. (page 250)

star (stär) A big ball of hot gas. **Stars** shine brightly in the night sky. (pages 319, 324)

stem (stem) The part of a plant that carries water to the leaves. The rose's **stem** has sharp thorns. (page 68)

Sun (sun) A big ball of hot gas that makes the day sky bright. The light from the **Sun** warms the Earth. (page 319)

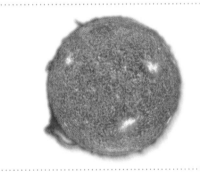

 T

tadpole (tad′pōl′) A very young frog. Rosie caught **tadpoles** in the pond. (page 87)

technology (tek nol′ə jē) The use of scientific knowledge to solve problems. A computer is a machine that uses **technology**. (page 343)

telescope (tel′ə skōp) A tool that makes things that are far away look closer and brighter. We use a **telescope** to look at the stars in the sky. (page 324)

temperature (tem′per ə chər) How hot or cold something is. The **temperature** can be very hot in the desert. (page 184)

thermometer (thər mom′ə tər) A tool that measures temperature. We looked at the **thermometer** to see how cold it was outside. (page 184)

vibrate (vī′brāt) To move back and forth very fast. The banjo strings **vibrate** to make sounds. (page 260)

water vapor (wȯ′tər vā′pər) A form of water in the air. You cannot see **water vapor**. (page 186)

weather (weŦH′ ər) What it is like outside. I like to make snowmen when the **weather** outside is cold and snowy. (page 183)

weathering (weŦH′ər ing) The breaking apart and changing of rocks. **Weathering** can change the shape, size, and color of rocks. (page 158)

wedge (wej) A simple machine used to push things apart. The farmer used a shovel as a **wedge** to break up the soil. (page 356)

wetland (wet′land′) A habitat that is covered with water. Tanya saw a bullfrog when she visited the **wetland** near her home. (page 34)

wheel and axle (hwēl and ak′səl) A simple machine used to move things. A wheelbarrow has a **wheel and axle**. (page 356)

Index

This index lists the pages on which topics appear in this book.
Page number after a *p* refer to a photograph or drawing.

Credits

Text

"The Frog on the Log" by Ilo Orleans from *Read-Aloud Rhymes for the Very Young* selected by Jack Prelutsky. Copyright ©1986 by Alfred A. Knopf.

"Wind" from *Some Folks Like Cats and Other Poems* by Ivy O. Eastwick. Reprinted by permission of Boyds Mills Press.

"Merry-Go-Round" from *I Like Machinery* by Dorothy Baruch.

"Taking Off" from *Very Young Verses*, edited by Barbara Peck Geismer and Antoinette Brown Suter. Copyright ©1945 by Houghton Mifflin company; Copyright ©Renewed 1972 by Barbara P. Geismer and Antoinette Brown Suter. Reprinted by permission of Houghton Mifflin Company. All Rights Reserved.

Illustrations

31–32, 34, 36, 38 Robert Hynes; 108–109 Cheryl Mendenhall; 322 Henk Dawson.

Photographs

Every effort has been made to secure permission and provide appropriate credit for photographic material. The publisher deeply regrets any omission and pledges to correct errors called to its attention in subsequent editions.

Unless otherwise acknowledged, all photographs are the property of Scott Foresman, a division of Pearson Education.

Photo locators denoted as follows: Top (T), Center (C), Bottom (B), Left (L), Right (R), Background (Bkgd).

Cover: (C) ©Tui De Roy/Minden Pictures, (Bkgd) ©Tim Davis/Corbis, (BL) Getty Images.

Front Matter: ii ©DK Images; iii (TR, B) ©DK Images; v ©DK Images; vi (B) ©DK Images, (CL) Corbis; vii Getty Images; viii (CL) Digital Vision, (BC) ©DK Images; ix (CR) ©Michael and Patricia Fogden/Corbis, (B) ©DK Images; x (TL, CL, B) ©Michael & Patricia Fogden/Corbis, (BR) ©Rick and Nora Bowers/Visuals Unlimited; xii (CL) ©Richard Price/Getty Images, (CL) ©Thomas Kitchin/Tom Stack & Associates, Inc.; xiii (CR) Stephen Oliver/©DK Images, (CR) Getty Images; xiv (CL) Getty Images, (B) ©DK Images; xv ©Frank Siteman/PhotoEdit; xvi ©Stone/Getty Images; xvii Courtesy of the London Toy and Model Museum/Paddington, London/©DK Images; xviii (CL) NASA Image Exchange, (CL) ©Roger Ressmeyer/Corbis; xix ©Lowell Georgia/Corbis; xx ©DK Images; xxii ©Douglas Faulkner/Photo Researchers, Inc.; xxiii ©William Harrigan/Lonely Planet Images; xxiv ©William Harrigan/Lonely Planet Images; xxv (BC) ©John Pontier/Animals Animals/Earth Scenes, (TR) ©Ames/NASA; xxix ©Ed Bock/Corbis; xxxi ©Little Blue Wolf Productions/Corbis; xxxii ©Andy Crawford/DK Images.

Unit A: Divider: ©Wayne R. Bilenduke/Getty Images; 1 (C) ©Sumio Harada/Minden Pictures, (TR) ©Royalty-Free/Corbis; 2 (B) Corbis, (T) ©Pat O'Hara/Corbis; 3 ©Mary Kate Denny/PhotoEdit; 5 (Bkgd) ©Pat O'Hara/Corbis, (C) ©Royalty-Free/Corbis, (TR) ©DK Images; 6 ©Pat O'Hara/Corbis; 7 (BR) ©Darrell Gulin/Corbis, (TR) ©DK Images; 8 (TR) ©Photowood, Inc./Corbis, (TL) Getty Images; 9 (TL) ©Manoj Shah/Animals Animals/Earth Scenes, (BR) ©J. & B. Photographers/Animals Animals/Earth Scenes; 10 (BL) ©Roy Morsch/Corbis, (TL) Digital Vision; 11 ©Guy Edwardes/Getty Images; 12 (BL) ©Darrell Gulin/Corbis, (C) Corbis, (TL) ©DK Images; 13 ©Dan Guravich/Corbis; 14 ©Mary Kate Denny/PhotoEdit; 16 (TL, C) ©DK Images; 17 Brand X Pictures; 20 (TL) ©Frank Lukasseck/Zefa/Corbis, (TR) ©Christine Schneider/Zefa/Corbis, (B) ©Don Mason/Corbis, (CL) ©IPS Co., Ltd./Beateworks; 21 (T,B) ©Royalty-Free/Corbis, (TC) ©DLILLC/Corbis; 22 (TC) ©Manoj Shah/Animals Animals/Earth Scenes, (B) ©J. & B. Photographers/Animals Animals/Earth Scenes; 23 (TR) ©Darrell Gulin/Corbis, (CL, C) ©DK Images; 24 (TL) Alan Schroeder/Courtesy of Sonia Ortega, (B) ©John Bova/Photo Researchers, Inc.; **Chapter 2:** 25 (C) Getty Images, (TR) ©Stephen Dalton/Photo Researchers, Inc.; 26 (C) ©W. Perry Conway/Corbis, (BL) ©Daniel J. Cox/Natural Exposures, (BR) ©David Samuel Robbins/Corbis; 27 (BR) ©Yva Momatiuk/John Eastcott/Minden Pictures, (BL) Digital Vision; 29 (Bkgd) ©W. Perry Conway/Corbis, (TR, C) ©DK Images; 30 ©W. Perry Conway/Corbis; 31 (BR) ©Taxi/Getty Images, (TR) ©Jeremy Thomas/Natural Visions; 32 (TL) ©Jeremy Thomas/Natural Visions, (BL) ©Jeffrey Lepore/Photo Researchers, Inc., (CR) ©Daniel J. Cox/Natural Exposures; 33 ©Daniel J. Cox/Natural Exposures; 34 (BC) ©Steve Maslowski/Photo Researchers, Inc., (TL) Brand X Pictures; 35 (C) ©David Samuel Robbins/Corbis, (BR) ©Joe McDonald/Corbis, (TR) ©Stone/Getty Images, (CR) Getty Images; 36 (CR) Digital Vision, (TL) ©Stone/Getty Images; 37 (CR) ©Flip Nicklin/Minden Pictures, (TR) Getty Images, (BR) ©Photographer's Choice/Getty Images; 38 (TL) ©Photographer's Choice/Getty Images, (BL) ©DK Images; 39 (BC) ©Yva Momatiuk/John Eastcott/Minden Pictures, (TC) ©Jose Fuste Raga/Corbis; 40 ©Yva Momatiuk/John Eastcott/Minden Pictures, (TR) ©Gerry Ellis/Minden Pictures; 42 (BC) ©Nigel J. Dennis/NHPA Limited, (T) ©Art Wolfe/Stone/Getty Images; 44 (TR, BR) ©Daniel J. Cox/Natural Exposures, (CL) ©David Samuel Robbins/Corbis, (CR) ©Yva Momatiuk/John Eastcott/Minden Pictures, (TR) Digital Vision; 45 (C) ©Robert Lubeck/Animals Animals/Earth Scenes, (TR) Brand X Pictures; 46 NASA; 47 (TR) Getty Images, (CL) ©Porterfield/Chickering/Photo Researchers, Inc., (BR) ©Doug Perrine/DRK Photo; 48 (BC) ©Operation Migration, Inc.; **Chapter 3:** 49 (TL) ©DK Images, (C) ©Michael Patrick O'Neill/NHPA Limited; 50 (BL) ©Richard K. LaVal/Animals Animals/Earth Scenes, (BR) ©T. Kitchin and V. Hurst/NHPA Limited, (C) Digital Vision; 51 (BR) ©Jeff Lepore/Photo Researchers, Inc., (BL) ©J.P. Ferrero/Jacana/Photo Researchers, Inc.; 53 (Bkgd) Digital Vision, (CL) Corel, (CR) ©Lynn Stone/Index Stock Imagery, (TR) ©Helen Williams/Photo Researchers, Inc.; ©54 David Fritts/Stone/Getty Images; 55 (BR) ©Steve Coombs/Photo Researchers, Inc., (TR) Getty Images; 56 (B) ©DK Images, (TL, C) ©B. Jones and M. Shimlock/NHPA Limited; 58 (TL, BL) ©Helen Williams/

Photo Researchers, Inc., (BR) ©DK Images; 59 ©Noboru Komine/Photo Researchers, Inc.; 60 (CR) ©Mitsuaki Iwago/Minden Pictures, (TR) Digital Vision, (B) ©S. Purdy Matthews/Stone/Getty Images, (TL) ©Ana Laura Gonzalez/Animals Animals/Earth Scenes; 61 ©Art Wolfe/Getty Images; 62 (BL) ©Stephen Krasemann/Stone, (CR) ©T. Kitchin and V. Hurst/NHPA Limited, (TL) ©Richard K. LaVal/Animals Animals/Earth Scenes; 63 (T) ©Richard K. LaVal/Animals Animals/Earth Scenes, (B) ©J.P. Ferrero/Jacana/Photo Researchers, Inc.; 64 (BC) ©Dante Fenolio/Photo Researchers, Inc., (TL, BC) ©DK Images; 65 (C) ©John Warden/Stone/Getty Images, (CR) ©Tom and Pat Leeson/Photo Researchers, Inc.; 66 (CR) ©DK Images, (TL) ©Jerry Young/©DK Images, (CL) ©Virginia Neefus/Animals Animals/Earth Scenes; 67 ©Chase Swift/Corbis; 70 (BR) ©Tom & Pat Leeson/Photo Researchers, Inc., (CL) Getty Images, (TL, CR) ©DK Images, (BL) ©Alan and Sandy Carey/Getty Images; 71 (CL) ©John Eastcott and Yva Momatiuk/NGS Image Collection, (BL) ©Ed Reschke/Peter Arnold, Inc., (CR, BR) ©DK Images; 72 (TL, C) ©DK Images; 73 (C, CR) ©DK Images; 74 (TR) ©H. H./Getty Images, (TC) Getty Images; 76 (Bkgd) ©Arctic National Wildlife Refuge/Getty Images, (CR) ©Art Wolfe/Getty Images, (B) ©S. Purdy Matthews/Stone/Getty Images; 77 (CR) ©Virginia Neefus/Animals Animals/Earth Scenes, (TR, BR) ©DK Images, (CR) ©Stephen Krasemann/Stone, (CC) ©Helen Williams/Photo Researchers, Inc.; 78 (CR) ©J.P. Ferrero/Jacana/Photo Researchers, Inc., (BR) ©Darrell Gulin/Corbis, (C) ©DK Images; 79 (C) Photo 24/Brand X Pictures, (CR) ©Ralph A. Clevenger/Corbis, (TR) ©DK Images; 80 (BL) ©JSC/NASA, (BR, Bkgd) NASA; **Chapter 4:** 81 ©Allen Russell/Index Stock Imagery; 82 (TL, C, BL) ©DK Images, (BR) ©Michael and Patricia Fogden/Corbis; 83 (BR) ©David Young-Wolff/PhotoEdit, (CR, BC) ©DK Images, (BL) ©George D. Lepp/Corbis; 85 (TR, C, CL) ©DK Images, (CR) Odds Farm Park/©DK Images, (Bkgd) ©Stephen Dalton/NHPA Limited; 86 ©Stephen Dalton/NHPA Limited; 87 (TR, CR, BR) ©DK Images; 88 (TL, C, B) ©DK Images; 89 ©DK Images; 90 (TR, B) ©DK Images, (TL) ©Geoff Brightling/©DK Images; 91 ©DK Images; 92 (T) ©George D. Lepp/Corbis, (B) ©Michael and Patricia Fogden/Corbis, (TL) ©DK Images; 93 (BL) George D. Lepp/Corbis, (T) ©DK Images; 94 (CR) ©T. Wiewandt/DRK Photo, (B) ©Joseph T. Collins/Photo Researchers, Inc., (TL) ©DK Images; 95 (TL) ©Jane Burton/Bruce Coleman, Inc., (C) ©Norbert Wu/Minden Pictures; 96 (BL) ©Pam Francis/Getty Images, (CR) ©Pat Doyle/Corbis; 97 (TR) ©George D. Lepp/Corbis, (B) ©Bruce Ando/Index Stock Imagery; 98 Derek Hall/©DK Images; 99 ©DK Images; 100 (TL) Matthew Ward/©DK Images, (BL) ©David Young-Wolff/PhotoEdit; 101 (BR) ©Bill Ross/Corbis, (TC) ©DK Images; 102 (B) ©DK Images, (CL) ©A. Riedmiller/Peter Arnold, Inc.; 103 ©DK Images; 104 (CL, CC, CR) Brand X Pictures, (BL, BR) ©DK Images; 105 (TR) ©Stephen Dalton/Photo Researchers, Inc., (B) ©Royalty-Free/Corbis; 106 ©Steve Terrill/Corbis; 110 (TR) ©David Young-Wolff/PhotoEdit, (TC) ©George D. Lepp/Corbis, (CL) ©Michael and Patricia Fogden/Corbis, (TL, CR) ©DK Images, (BR) ©Nicolas Granier/Peter Arnold, Inc.; 111 (TR) ©DK Images, (CL, CR) ©Jeff Foott/Bruce Coleman Collection, (C) ©Daniel W. Gotshall/Seapics; 112 ©Ed Bock/Corbis; **Chapter 5:** 113 (C) ©Jonathan Blair/Corbis, (TR) ©David Aubrey/Corbis,

(BC) ©Clive Druett/Papilio/Corbis; 114 (BR) ©Gary Braasch/Corbis, (C) ©Michael & Patricia Fogden/Corbis, (T) ©Ken Lucas/Visuals Unlimited; 115 ©Hal Horwitz/Corbis; 117 (C) Getty Images, (TR, Bkgd) ©Michael & Patricia Fogden/Corbis; 118 ©Michael & Patricia Fogden/Corbis; 119 ©Michael & Patricia Fogden/Minden Pictures; 122 (B, BL) ©Michael & Patricia Fogden/Corbis, (TL) ©Michael Fogden/Animals Animals/Earth Scenes, (BR) ©Rick and Nora Bowers/Visuals Unlimited; 123 ©Kevin Schafer/NHPA Limited; 124 (TL) ©Michael & Patricia Fogden/Corbis, (BL) ©Kevin Schafer/NHPA Limited, (B) ©Steve Kaufman/Corbis; 125 (C) ©Rick and Nora Bowers/Visuals Unlimited, (CR) ©Kevin Schafer/NHPA Limited, (BR) ©Michael & Patricia Fogden/Corbis, (TR) ©Steve Kaufman/Corbis; 126 (B) ©Sue A. Thompson/Visuals Unlimited, (TL) ©Royalty-Free/Corbis; 127 ©David A. Northcott/Corbis; 128 (C) ©David A. Northcott/Corbis, (TC) ©Rick Poley/Visuals Unlimited, (TL) ©David A. Ponton/Mira, (TR) ©William J. Weber/Visuals Unlimited, (B) ©Sue A. Thompson/Visuals Unlimited; 129 (TC) ©Ted Levin/Animals Animals/Earth Scenes, (TL) ©Royalty-Free/Corbis, (CR) ©James Allen/Bruce Coleman, Inc.; 132 (TC) ©Michael & Patricia Fogden/Corbis, (C) ©John Shaw/Tom Stack & Associates, Inc.; 133 (TL) ©Michael & Patricia Fogden/Corbis, (CL) ©John Gerlach/Visuals Unlimited, (C) ©Tim Wright/Corbis, (C) ©William J. Weber/Visuals Unlimited, (CR) Getty Images, (CR) ©Michael Sewell/Peter Arnold, Inc., (CL) ©DK Images; 134 (TR, CL, C) ©Michael & Patricia Fogden/Corbis, (CR) ©Rick and Nora Bowers/Visuals Unlimited, (CR) ©Kevin Schafer/NHPA Limited, (TC) ©Hal Horwitz/Corbis, (BR) ©Jonathan Blair/Corbis; 135 (TR) ©David Aubrey/Corbis, (CR) Getty Images; 136 (BL) ©Kate Bennett Mendz/Animals Animals/Earth Scenes, (T, TC, C, R) Jerry Young/©DK Images, (TL, CR, CL, BR) ©DK Images; 138 (TL) ©Pat O'Hara/Corbis, (CL) ©W. Perry Conway/Corbis, (CL) ©David Fritts/Stone/Getty Images, (CL) ©Stephen Dalton/NHPA Limited, (BL) ©Michael & Patricia Fogden/Corbis; 140 ©Ian Beames/Ecoscene/Corbis; 142 ©John Watkins/Frank Lane Picture Agency/Corbis; 144 (Bkgd) ©Gerry Ellis/Minden Pictures, (TC) ©Breck P. Kent/Animals Animals/Earth Scenes, (BC) Corbis.

Unit B: Divider: ©Hiroyuki Matsumoto/Getty Images; **Chapter 6:** 145 (C) ©Steve Raymer/NGS Image Collection, (BR) ©Paul Chesley/NGS Image Collection; 146 (TL, BL) ©Barry L. Runk/Grant Heilman Photography, (BR) ©Garry D. McMichael/Photo Researchers, Inc., (CR) ©Richard Price/Getty Images, (CL) ©DK Images; 147 ©DK Images; 149 (Bkgd) ©Richard Price/Getty Images, (C) NASA; 150 ©Richard Price/Getty Images; 151 ©Thomas Kitchin/Tom Stack & Associates, Inc.; 152 (TR) Silver Burdett Ginn, (BR) ©J. Jangoux/Photo Researchers, Inc., (TL) ©Calvin Larsen/Photo Researchers, Inc., (C) ©Craig Aurness/Corbis; 153 ©Steve Dunwell/Getty Images; 154 (TL, B) ©DK Images; 155 (TL) ©Galen Rowell/Corbis, (TR) ©W. Perry Conway/Corbis, (B) ©J. Eastcott Film/NGS Image Collection; 156 (BL) ©J. P. Ferrero/Jacana/Photo Researchers, Inc., (BR) Getty Images, (C, CR) ©Barry L. Runk/Grant Heilman Photography, (TL, TC) ©DK Images; 157 ©Steve Shott/DK Images; 158 ©DK Images; 159 (TR) ©Barry L. Runk/Grant Heilman Photography, (TL) ©Michael

Marten/Photo Researchers, Inc., (BL) ©Garry D. McMichael/ Photo Researchers, Inc., (BR) ©Jeffrey Greenberg/Photo Researchers, Inc.; 160 (TL) Brand X Pictures, (BC) ©Jim Erickson/Corbis; 161 (B) ©Philip James Corwin/Corbis, (T) ©Royalty-Free/Corbis; 162 Getty Image; 163 (CL) ©Image Source Limited, (CR) ©Cosmo Condina/Getty Images; 164 (TR) ©Jim Craigmyle/Corbis, (CR) ©Michael T. Sedam/ Corbis, (CR) ©DK Images, (BR) ©David R. Frazier/Photo Researchers, Inc., (TL) ©Alan Kearney/Getty Images; 165 ©Royalty-Free/Corbis; 170 ©Stone/Getty Images; 172 (TR, C, CR) ©Barry L. Runk/Grant Heilman Photography, (TC) ©Garry D. McMichael/Photo Researchers, Inc., (CL) ©DK Images, (CR) ©J. Eastcott Film/NGS Image Collection, (BR) ©Michael Marten/Photo Researchers, Inc.; 174 NASA; 175 (T) ©DK Images, (C) ©Francois Gohier/Photo Researchers, Inc.; 176 (Bkgd) ©John McAnulty/Corbis, (BL) ©Courtesy of the New York State Museum/Albany, NY, (CR) Petrified Sea Gardens, Inc.; **Chapter 7:** 177 ©Taxi/Getty Images; 178 ©Marc Muench/Corbis; 179 (BL) ©Paul A. Souders/ Corbis, (BR) ©Stone/Getty Images; 180 Getty Images; 181 (TR) ©Stephen Oliver/©DK Images, (C) ©Bob Burch/Index Stock Imagery, (Bkgd) ©Marc Muench/Corbis; 182 ©Marc Muench/Corbis; 183 ©Zefa Visual Media/Index Stock Imagery; 184 (BL) ©Nigel J. Dennis; Gallo Images/Corbis, (TL) ©Stone/Getty Images, (BR) ©Marc Muench/Corbis; 185 (BL) Getty Images, (BR) ©Bruce Peebles/Corbis, (BL) ©Stone/Getty Images; 186 ©John Mead/Photo Researchers, Inc.; 187 (TL) ©Jeff Foott/Bruce Coleman, Inc., (TR) ©John Mead/Photo Researchers, Inc., (BL) ©Paul A. Souders/ Corbis, (BR) ©Stone/Getty Images; 188 (TL, BR) ©Roy Morsch/Corbis, (TR) ©Maslowski Photo/Photo Researchers, Inc., (CR) Getty Images; 189 ©Stone/Getty Images; 190 (TL, B) ©Stone/Getty Images; 191 ©David Pollack/Corbis; 192 (TC) Matthew Ward/©DK Images, (TR) ©Everett Johnson/ Index Stock Imagery, (BL, BR) Getty Images, (CR) ©Stephen Oliver/©DK Images; 193 (BL, BR) Getty Images; 194 ©Royalty-Free/Corbis; 196 (C, CL) Getty Images; 197 (R, C, CL, CR) ©Bruce Peebles/Corbis; 198 (BR) ©DK Images, (TC) ©Stone/Getty Images, (C) ©Paul A. Souders/Corbis; 199 ©Stone/Getty Images; 200 (Bkgd) ©John Mead/Photo Researchers, Inc., (BL, BR) ©Goddard Space Flight Center/ NASA; 202 (B) ©Steve Shott/DK Images, (TL) ©Richard Price/Getty Images, (CL) ©Marc Muench/Corbis; 204 Getty Images; 206 Getty Images; 207 ©Stone/Getty Images; 208 (Bkgd) ©John McAnulty/Corbis, (Inset) ©David Young-Wolff/ PhotoEdit, (CL) Getty Images.

Unit C: Divider: (Bkgd) Masterfile Corporation; **Chapter 8:** 209 (C) ©Rob Lewine/Corbis; 210 Getty Images; 218 (TL, BL) ©DK Images; 219 ©DK Images; 221 ©DK Images; 234 ©Dan Gair/Index Stock Imagery; 236 (TL) ©DK Images, (TR) Getty Images; 237 ©DK Images; 238 (CR, BL, Bkgd) NASA; 240 (BR) ©Roger Schreiber/Courtesy of Chihuly Studio, (TR, C) ©Dale Chihuly/Sunset Tower (2003)/Terry Rishel/Courtesy of Chihuly Studio, ©Peter Yates/Corbis; **Chapter 9:** 241 Getty Images; 242 Getty Images; 245 Getty Images; 246 Getty Images; 247 ©Frank Siteman/ PhotoEdit; 248 (BL) ©Frank Siteman/PhotoEdit, (TL) Getty Images; 249 Getty Images; 250 Getty Images; 256 ©DK Images; 257 ©DK Images; 260 Getty Images, (TL, C) ©DK Images; 261 ©DK Images; 262 Getty Images; 263 ©Alan

Schein Photography/Corbis; 264 (B) Getty Images, (TL) ©Marcia W. Griffen/Animals Animals/Earth Scenes; 265 (BL) ©George F. Mobley/NGS Image Collection, (TR) ©Jeff Greenberg/PhotoEdit, (TL) ©John Cancalosi/Peter Arnold, Inc., (BR) ©Dennis MacDonald/PhotoEdit; 266 ©Surgi Stock/Getty Images; 268 (CL) Digital Vision, (C) Getty Images, (C) ©DK Images, (BC) ©Ron Kimball/PhotoLibrary, ©Comstock, Inc.; 269 (CL) ©Allsport Concepts/Getty Images, (C) ©Dean Abramson/Stock Boston, (CR) ©Johnson Space Center/NASA, (BC) ©Ron Kimball/PhotoLibrary, (C) Getty Images; 270 (TC, C) ©DK Images; 272 (Bkgd) ©Jeff Foott/Bruce Coleman, Inc., (TR) ©Time Life Pictures/NASA/ Getty Images, (CL) NASA; **Chapter 10:** 273 ©Owaki-Kulla/Corbis; 274 (BR) ©Philip James Corwin/Corbis, (BL) ©Holly Harris/Getty Images, (C) ©Jose Fuste Raga/Corbis; 277 (Bkgd) ©Jose Fuste Raga/Corbis, ©David Brooke/ Corbis; 278 ©Onne van der Wal/Corbis; 279 (TR) ©Jose Fuste Raga/Corbis, (BR) Getty Images; 280 (BC) ©Ric Ergenbright/Corbis, (CR) ©Phil Degginger/Color-Pic, Inc.; 282 ©Mark L. Stephenson/Corbis; 283 (C, Bkgd) ©Royalty-Free/Corbis; 284 ©Royalty-Free/Corbis; 285 (T) ©Royalty-Free/Corbis, (B) ©E. R. Degginger/Photo Researchers, Inc.; 286 Getty Images; 287 ©Royalty-Free/Corbis, (TR) Getty Images; 288 ©David Young-Wolff/PhotoEdit; 290 ©Steve Raymer/NGS Image Collection; 291 (T, BL) Getty Images; 293 Courtesy of the London Toy and Model Museum/ Paddington, London/©DK Images; 294 Getty Images; 297 (BL) ©Stone/Getty Images, (TL, BR) Getty Images, ©George Shelley/Corbis; 298 ©Andrea Olsheskie/Getty Images; 302 (CR) ©Holly Harris/Getty Images, (TR) ©Ric Ergenbright/ Corbis, (BR) ©Angelo Cavalli/Age Fotostock; 303 Courtesy of the London Toy and Model Museum/Paddington, London/ ©DK Images; 304 (Bkgd) ©Emilio De Cesaris/Stone/Getty Images, (BL) Kennedy Space Center/NASA, ©Emilio De Cesaris/Stone/Getty Images; 305 ©Dave King/DK Images; 306 (CL) Getty Images, (CL) ©Jose Fuste Raga/Corbis; 308 ©DK Images; 310 ©Sandy Felsenthal/Corbis; 312 (B) Dave King/©DK Images, (Bkgd) Getty Images.

Unit D: Divider: ©NASA/Roger Ressmeyer/Corbis; **Chapter 11:** 313 ©Dale C. Spartas/Corbis; 314 ©John McAnulty/Corbis; 315 (BR) ©DK Images, (BL) ©NASA/ Omni-Photo Communications, Inc., (BR) ©Roger Ressmeyer/ Corbis; 317 (C) NASA, (Bkgd) ©John McAnulty/Corbis, (TR) NASA Image Exchange; 318 ©John McAnulty/Corbis; 319 (TR) Kim Taylor/©DK Images, (CR) NASA; 320 (BL) Corbis, (TL) ©Barbra Leigh/Corbis, (TL) ©Mark Antman/The Image Works, Inc., (TL) ©John Henley/Corbis, (TR) ©Richard Glover/Ecoscene/Corbis; 321 ©Richard Cummins/Corbis; 322 (C) ©Tibor Bognár/Corbis, (TL) NASA; 323 ©Royalty-Free/Corbis; 324 (BR) ©DK Images, (TL) ©Jeff Vanuga/ Corbis; 325 (CL) ©Roger Ressmeyer/Corbis, (CR) ©Jerry Lodriguss/Photo Researchers, Inc.; 326 (TL) ©Dennis di Cicco/Corbis, (CL) ©Jet Propulsion Laboratory/NASA; 327 (C) ©Johnson Space Center/NASA, (TC) ©Jeff Vanuga/ Corbis, (TL, TC) ©Dennis di Cicco/Corbis; 328 ©Allan Davey/Masterfile Corporation; 330 (C) ©Stone/Getty Images, (CR, BR) Getty Images; 332 (TC) ©DK Images, (CR) ©Jeff Vanuga/Corbis, (TR) ©Denis Scott/Corbis, (C) ©NASA/Omni-Photo Communications, Inc., (BR) ©Robert W. Madden/NGS Image Collection; 333 (TR) Getty Images,

(TR) NASA Image Exchange; 334 (BL) ©John F. Kennedy Space Center/NASA Image Exchange, (CL, CR, BR) NASA Image Exchange; 335 (CL) ©J. Silver/SuperStock, (CR) ©Jet Propulsion Laboratory/NASA Image Exchange; 336 (CR) NASA Image Exchange, (BL) ©JSC/NASA; **Chapter 12:** 337 ©Peter Beck/Corbis; 338 Getty Images; 339 (CR) ©Francesco Ruggeri/Getty Images, (TR, BR) ©Royalty-Free/Corbis, (BL) ©DK Images; 342 ©Randy Wells/Corbis; 343 (BR) ©DK Images, (TR) ©Tom Grill/Age Fotostock; 344 ©Sylvain Saustier/Corbis; 345 ©Eric and David Hosking/Corbis; 346 Getty Images; 347 (BR) ©Stone/Getty Images, (BL) ©Lowell Georgia/Corbis; 352 (TL) ©David R. Frazier Photolibrary, (B) ©Grant Heilman/Grant Heilman Photography; 353 ©Lester Lefkowitz/Corbis; 354 (BL) ©David R. Frazier Photolibrary, (BR) ©Jeremy Hoare/Getty Images, (TL) ©R. Francis/Robert Harding Picture Library, Ltd.; 355 (BL, BR) ©David R. Frazier Photolibrary; 356 (CR) ©Susan Van Etten/PhotoEdit, (TR) ©Darwin Wiggett/Corbis; 358 (CL, CR) ©Royalty-Free/Corbis, (TR) ©DK Images, (BR) ©Francesco Ruggeri/Getty Images; 359 (T) ©Royalty-Free/Corbis, (TR) ©DK Images; 360 (TR) ©David Young-Wolff/PhotoEdit, (BR) ©Kent Warwick/PhotoLibrary; 361 ©Mary Fran Loftus/Omni-Photo Communications, Inc.; 366 (BC) ©Francesco Ruggeri/Getty Images, (TR, BR) ©DK Images, (TC, CC) ©Royalty-Free/Corbis; 368 (B, Bkgd) ©NASA Ames, Dominic Hart/NASA; 369 Corbis; 370 (B) ©Sylvain Saustier/Corbis, (TL) ©John McAnulty/Corbis; 372 ©DK Images; 374 (C) ©Museum of Flight/Corbis, (B) Getty Images; 375 Getty Images; 376 Getty Images.

End Matter: EM2 (TC, CR, BC) ©DK Images, (TR) ©Lynn Stone/Index Stock Imagery; EM3 (TR) ©T. Kitchin and V. Hurst/NHPA Limited, (BR) ©Paul A. Souders/Corbis; EM4 (TC) ©Bruce Ando/Index Stock Imagery, (BR) Getty Images, (TR) ©Yva Momatiuk/John Eastcott/Minden Pictures; EM5 (CR) Getty Images, (CR) ©Mark L. Stephenson/Corbis, (BR) ©Garry D. McMichael/Photo Researchers, Inc.; EM6 (CL) ©Kevin Schafer/NHPA Limited, (TCR, CR) ©Michael & Patricia Fogden/Corbis, (TCL) ©Steve Kaufman/Corbis, (BC) ©Rick and Nora Bowers/Visuals Unlimited, (B) Getty Images; EM7 (TC) ©Holly Harris/Getty Images, (BR) ©Dennis MacDonald/PhotoEdit, (TR) ©W. Perry Conway/Corbis, (BR) Getty Images; EM8 (CR) ©Ric Ergenbright/Corbis, (BR) ©Barry L. Runk/Grant Heilman Photography, (TR) ©Daniel J. Cox/Natural Exposures; EM9 (CR) ©Royalty-Free/Corbis, (BR) ©Michael and Patricia Fogden/Corbis; EM10 (CR) ©DK Images, (CR) ©Royalty-Free/Corbis; EM11 (CR) ©Sue A. Thompson/Visuals Unlimited, (TR) ©Darrell Gulin/Corbis; EM12 (CR) ©Jeff Vanuga/Corbis, (CR) ©Galen Rowell/Corbis, (TR) ©DK Images, (BR) ©Mary Kate Denny/PhotoEdit; EM13 (CR) ©NASA/Omni-Photo Communications, Inc., (TR) Digital Vision; EM14 (TR) ©Jeff Foott/Bruce Coleman, Inc., (CR) ©Francesco Ruggeri/Getty Images, (BR) ©George D. Lepp/Corbis; EM15 (TR) ©Gary Braasch/Corbis, (CR) ©DK Images, (CR) ©J. Eastcott Film/NGS Image Collection; EM16 (C) ©David Pollack/Corbis, (BR) Derek Hall/©DK Images, (TC, TR, BC) ©DK Images; EM17 (BR) ©Stone/Getty Images, (BR) ©DK Images, (CR) Corbis; EM18 (CR) NASA, (BR) ©DK Images, (TR) ©Roger Ressmeyer/Corbis; EM19 (BC) ©Nigel J. Dennis/Gallo Images/Corbis, (CR) ©DK Images; EM20 (TR) Getty Images, (BR) ©Michael Marten/Photo Researchers, Inc., (CR) ©Zefa Visual Media/Index Stock Imagery; EM21 David Samuel Robbins/Corbis

End Sheet: ©Frans Lanting/Minden Pictures